Living to Please God

Gordon and Theresa
Ferguson

About the authors: Gordon and Theresa graduated together from Northwestern State University in the field of education and Gordon received his master's degree from Harding School of Theology. With more than fifty years of experience in ministry each, Gordon has served in various roles, as has Theresa. His focus has been Bible  teaching and writing, and hers has been the teaching and spiritual counseling of women. Gordon has written twenty books, and this is their first coauthored book. They will celebrate their 60th wedding anniversary on January 30, 2025 and currently make their home in McKinney, Texas. For additional information about their work and ministry, go to GordonFerguson.org. All of Gordon's books are available at www.ipibooks.com.

ILLUMINATION **IP**
PUBLISHERS

www.ipibooks.com

CONTENTS

Section One
Character Studies

Section Two
Victorious Christian Living

CONTENTS

Section Two

Victorious Christian Living (continued)

Section Three

Additional Studies

Living to Please God

¹As for other matters, brothers and sisters, we instructed you how to live in order to please God, as in fact you are living. Now we ask you and urge you in the Lord Jesus to do this more and more. ²For you know what instructions we gave you by the authority of the Lord Jesus.

³It is God's will that you should be sanctified: that you should avoid sexual immorality; ⁴that each of you should learn to control your own body a in a way that is holy and honorable, ⁵not in passionate lust like the pagans, who do not know God; ⁶and that in this matter no one should wrong or take advantage of a brother or sister. The Lord will punish all those who commit such sins, as we told you and warned you before. ⁷For God did not call us to be impure, but to live a holy life. ⁸Therefore, anyone who rejects this instruction does not reject a human being but God, the very God who gives you his Holy Spirit.

⁹Now about your love for one another we do not need to write to you, for you yourselves have been taught by God to love each other. ¹⁰And in fact, you do love all of God's family throughout Macedonia. Yet we urge you, brothers and sisters, to do so more and more, ¹¹and to make it your ambition to lead a quiet life: You should mind your own business and work with your hands, just as we told you, ¹²so that your daily life may win the respect of outsiders and so that you will not be dependent on anybody.

—1 Thessalonians 4:1-12

SECTION ONE

Character Studies

13All these people were still living by faith when they died. They did not receive the things promised; they only saw them and welcomed them from a distance, admitting that they were foreigners and strangers on earth. 14People who say such things show that they are looking for a country of their own. 15If they had been thinking of the country they had left, they would have had opportunity to return. 16Instead, they were longing for a better country—a heavenly one. Therefore God is not ashamed to be called their God, for he has prepared a city for them.

—Hebrews 11:13-16

CHAPTER ONE

Joshua: Victory through Leadership
Part 1

—Gordon Ferguson

"Be strong and courageous, because you will lead these people to inherit the land I swore to their ancestors to give them." (Joshua 1:6)

The conquest of Canaan by the Israelites under the leadership of Joshua was nothing short of spectacular. These people had been on a 40-year death march, living as nomads in lands not their own. They watched as their older friends and relatives died out one-by-one. While all these events produced a healthy fear of God, the Israelites were still unprepared for what was to come. Ultimately, they were supremely victorious due to several key reasons. They enjoyed victory through great leadership, faith, and strenuous warfare. This chapter and the next two will focus on one of these elements of victory.

Without question, the leadership of Joshua provided an absolutely essential ingredient in the conquest of Canaan. There are no great movements without great leaders. When God moves, he always moves through those whom he calls to lead. Anyone who has a fear of highly influential leadership ultimately has a fear of God and his purposes. Joshua was a leader of high impact whose influence outlived him. A suitable epitaph for his tombstone would have been Joshua 24:31: "Israel served the Lord throughout the lifetime of Joshua and of the elders who outlived him and who had experienced everything the Lord had done for Israel."

Joshua was a great leader because he was a *discipled* leader. Powerful leaders are developed, not simply born. The world is full of people with tremendous leadership potential who never become respected, influential leaders. The ones most willing to follow and learn from accomplished leaders are most likely to become leaders themselves. Joshua served in the background for many years before he became the ultimate leader himself. He was content to simply be known as the *"young aide"* of Moses (Exodus 33:11).

The blossoming leader who serves to exalt himself will be resisted by God, but the one who humbles himself will be raised up by God. Joshua was a submissive learner before he was an influential leader. This was the same message that the Apostle Peter expressed when he wrote: "In the same way, you who are younger, submit yourselves to your elders. All of you, clothe yourselves with humility toward one another, because, 'God opposes the proud but shows favor to the humble.' Humble yourselves, therefore, under God's mighty hand, that he may lift you up in due time" (1 Peter 5:5-6).

He also was a great leader because he was a *secure* leader. He was not out to prove or advance himself. When reading through the book of Joshua, one is impressed with his constant focus on God and with how he served his predecessor Moses. He was secure in the overall leadership of God. He was secure in his training under Moses. He knew who he was and felt totally secure in that knowledge. Because of this security in leadership, he was neither threatened nor intimidated by other strong leaders like Caleb. Insecure leaders cannot effectively lead other leaders, and therefore they can never effectively raise up new leaders of real strength. Unless we can accept who we are, rather than worrying about who we are not, our leadership will be consistently insecure and weak.

Joshua was an outstanding leader because he was a *confrontational* leader. He and Caleb were willing to confront an entire nation of negative unbelievers who were highly emotional at the time. As you read these passages, you can see how the faith of Joshua and Caleb empowered them to stand up against an unfaithful nation after spying out the land.

Numbers 13:26-31

[26] They came back to Moses and Aaron and the whole Israelite community at Kadesh in the Desert of Paran. There they

reported to them and to the whole assembly and showed them the fruit of the land. [27] They gave Moses this account: "We went into the land to which you sent us, and it does flow with milk and honey! Here is its fruit.

[28] But the people who live there are powerful, and the cities are fortified and very large. We even saw descendants of Anak there. [29] The Amalekites live in the Negev; the Hittites, Jebusites and Amorites live in the hill country; and the Canaanites live near the sea and along the Jordan." [30] Then Caleb silenced the people before Moses and said, "We should go up and take possession of the land, for we can certainly do it." [31] But the men who had gone up with him said, "We can't attack those people; they are stronger than we are."

Numbers 14:1-10

[1] That night all the members of the community raised their voices and wept aloud. [2] All the Israelites grumbled against Moses and Aaron, and the whole assembly said to them, "If only we had died in Egypt! Or in this wilderness! [3] Why is the LORD bringing us to this land only to let us fall by the sword? Our wives and children will be taken as plunder. Wouldn't it be better for us to go back to Egypt?" [4] And they said to each other, "We should choose a leader and go back to Egypt." [5] Then Moses and Aaron fell facedown in front of the whole Israelite assembly gathered there. [6] Joshua son of Nun and Caleb son of Jephunneh, who were among those who had explored the land, tore their clothes [7] and said to the entire Israelite assembly, "The land we passed through and explored is exceedingly good. [8] If the LORD is pleased with us, he will lead us into that land, a land flowing with milk and honey, and will give it to us. [9] Only do not rebel against the LORD. And do not be afraid of the people of the land, because we will devour them. Their protection is gone, but the LORD is with us. Do not be afraid of them." [10] But the whole assembly talked about stoning them...

Although Joshua and Caleb were nearly stoned to death, they boldly stood up for God. When Joshua became the leader of the nation, he gave specific orders and not general suggestions. He was not afraid to confront issues and expose hearts. Up to and including his farewell address, he consistently laid out the consequences of sin and righteousness, never hesitating to challenge the Israelites' tendency to rebel. Although harshness and bossiness are never to be a part of godly leadership, one cannot be a godly leader without being direct and challenging. When sin is not confronted, hearts are not challenged; and because hearts are not challenged, discipling does not occur. Leaders of impact are those who crucify the fleshly tendency to avoid conflict.

Finally, Joshua was a tremendous leader because he was an *inspirational* leader. He inspired people by his personal example. He was not an armchair general or administrator. He was with the people in the midst of the battle. He led by doing, not simply by commanding. And he set the pace by confronting the top leaders of his day who were opposing the Israelite's goal of occupying the promised land (Joshua 10:16-28). He was not content to merely join in the battle; he sought to establish himself as a leader among the nations who were opposing the Israelites. Had he lived in our day, he would have sought to influence leaders and show them the nature of the God we serve.

Because Joshua had a personal example to back him up, he was able to inspire by his words as well as his actions. His speaking was characterized by two things: encouragement to be strong and courageous, and reminders of God's leadership in every event or aspect of their lives. We, too, can be strong and courageous. Then, and only then, can God use us to advance his kingdom and go where no one has yet had the faith to go!

QUESTIONS FOR THOUGHT

1. Do you get discipled (mentored) in your leadership role? Do you have someone in your life who is helping you grow in humility as you grow in your boldness?

2. Are you secure in your role of leadership? Are you secure in leading your group to make an impact for God in your community?

3. Do you have the courage to confront apathy in your church or Bible study group?

ACTION ITEMS

Walk with other leaders and find men who inspire you. Learn what their greatest skills are that will enable you to inspire the disciples in your group!

CHAPTER TWO

Joshua: Victory through Faith
Part 2

—Gordon Ferguson

"There has never been a day like it before or since, a day when the Lord listened to a human being. Surely the Lord was fighting for Israel." (Joshua 10:14)

In the first chapter of this series, victory through *leadership* was discussed. The focus of this second installment will be on victory through *faith*. Without faith, we can neither please God nor finish the task he has given us of taking the world for Christ. The letter of Hebrews reminds us: "And without faith it is impossible to please God, because anyone who comes to him must believe that he exists and that he rewards those who earnestly seek him" (Hebrews 11:6). The examples of faith we find in the book of Joshua are worthy of imitation as we look to them for inspiration to fulfill the tasks that God has given us.

When we read the first chapter of Joshua, one thing about faith becomes clear: it is not easy to obtain. Even such a "spiritual giant" as Joshua had to be urged by both God and his followers to have faith, and to be strong and courageous. His tendency, as with most humans facing great obstacles, was to become fearful and lose his confidence (Joshua 1:9)! Joshua had to have a word from God to help him overcome his fear. God said: "Be strong and courageous, because you will lead these people to inherit the land I swore to their ancestors to give them" (Joshua 1:6). God then proceeded to ask Joshua to take it to the next level. He said: "Be strong and *very* courageous" (Joshua 1:7). He reiterates it again in verse 9: "Have I not commanded you? Be strong and courageous. Do not be afraid; do not be discouraged, for the Lord your God will be with you wherever you go" (Joshua 1:9). God had to repeat it four times in short succession: *"Be strong and courageous."* To move from fear to faith, Joshua had to make the decision to be ruled by God rather than by his emotions. Once made, he stuck with that decision for a lifetime.

While the entire reign of Joshua could be viewed as an example of great faith, perhaps the most inspiring act of faith is found in chapter 10. This account teaches us some powerful lessons about "world-shaking" faith.

First, their faith was a *working* faith. The army marched all night, fought all day, and then fought another full day while the sun stopped in the middle of the sky (Joshua 10:9-13). Praying for a miracle after we have done all that we can is one thing. Praying for a miracle to compensate for a lack of work is yet another.

Along with the command to engage the Amorites, part of the impetus was to remember that God was with them. The Lord said to Joshua: "Do not be afraid of them; I have given them into your hand. Not one of them will be able to withstand you" (Joshua 10:8). We must constantly remind ourselves that God is fighting on our behalf.

God will honor such prayers! He has never rewarded laziness; and he has never failed to reward diligence. Just how hard are you willing to work to bring people to faith in Christ? The answer to that question is easy—just as hard as you are presently working! Remember the words of James: "What good is it, my brothers and sisters, if someone claims to have faith but has no deeds? Can such faith save them? ...In the same way, faith by itself, if it is not accompanied by action, is dead" (James 2:14-17).

Second, faith is expressed in *powerful* prayers. The words of Joshua in verse 12 do not give the impression of a sweet little request. He shouted and cried out to God! Jesus did not only have "quiet times;" he had "loud times" (Hebrews 5:7). God answers those "who cry out to him day and night" (Luke 18:7)! Too many of us have weak faith because we have weak prayers. And I don't mean weak in time spent or even weak in content. The weakness is in the lack of urgency and conviction with which we make our requests. Replace a significant number of your "quiet times" with "loud times." Do not expect to move God without urgency and energy.

Third, faith is willing to make requests that are *publicly heard and yet humanly absurd.* Can you imagine asking for something like the sun and moon standing still in their place? Most of us don't have the courage to ask for blessings beyond what we have observed being given to others. In fact, we struggle in believing that God will give us what we have not received before. Therefore, the temptation to be filled with unbelief when asking for something that we've never seen or heard about is overwhelming. And yet Joshua made the request in the hearing of those he led.

In the early days of our movement, faith was stretched and strained repeatedly as things were attempted which had never been done before. Many other faith-challenging mountains are still before us. Multiplying disciples in locations where persecution takes lives has not been done since the early days of Christianity. It will take great faith to confess Jesus as Lord in the face of near-certain persecution or death.

Reaching out to our communities to saturate the area with the gospel to the point of seeing more people converted than we have ever seen before is another mountainous challenge to our faith. Seeing the majority of members in our local congregations actively involved in outreach and studying the Bible with people has not been true for years. Planting new churches inside and outside of America at rates not yet seen before would take money and volunteers at levels we cannot imagine. But if we had the faith of Joshua, anything is possible. Jesus said it was. Do we believe him? Are our hearts set on the same goals for the world like Jesus's heart was?

Yes, conquest for God is totally dependent on our having great faith and believing that he will use us to do the unthinkable. The impossible is possible with him, but the kingdom in the 2020s needs repentance and leaders like Joshua to advance. Such disciples respond to "it hasn't been done before" by saying "Amen! It's about time! Let's do it now!"

QUESTIONS FOR THOUGHT

1. Do you demonstrate your faith by action or are your victories all in the past?

2. As you take steps of faith in obedience to God, are they preceded by earnest prayer?

3. When was the last time you prayed an impossible prayer and how did God respond?

ACTION ITEMS

Gather the disciples in your small group and decide to do something you have never attempted before. (Perhaps door-knocking your entire neighborhood or apartment complex). Whatever it is, have faith that God will be with you and the Holy Spirit will empower you to accomplish it. Then, share the news of what happened with other small study groups in your church.

CHAPTER THREE

Joshua: Victory in Our Spiritual Warfare Part 3

—Gordon Ferguson

"The Lord has driven out before you great and powerful nations; to this day no one has been able to withstand you. One of you routs a thousand, because the Lord your God fights for you, just as he promised. So be very careful to love the Lord your God." (Joshua 23:9-11)

The fledgling nation of Israel moved from a weak position as rebellious wilderness wanderers to the strong position as conquerors of a rich land. Their victory came because of outstanding leadership, great faith, and a willingness to wage war on the enemies of God. The first two chapters in this series dealt with the subjects of leadership and faith, and this final one will focus on struggle.

The Old Testament is replete with physical examples which provide us spiritual applications so we can thrive in God's kingdom. For instance, the priests, garments, temple and sacrifices in the Old Testament have their spiritual counterparts in the New Testament. Surely God intended that physical warfare in the Old Testament would be used to inspire us to fight our spiritual battles with Satan and his demonic angels. Unless this was God's design, it would be difficult to explain why so much space was given to battle accounts.

Make no mistake about it, we are in a war to the death. If you have no sense of head-to-head struggle with Satan, you must be going in the same direction that he is! Like a friend of mine said, "If you think the Christian life is easy, you must not be living it." Revelation 12 and Ephesians 6, along with many other New Testament passages, make it abundantly clear that we do struggle mightily with the spiritual forces of evil in the spiritual realms. We must clearly understand that we are in a cosmic battle for our own souls and the souls of others. Paul made this clear to the Ephesian Christians.

Ephesians 6:10-18

[10] Finally, be strong in the Lord and in his mighty power. [11] Put on the full armor of God, so that you can take your stand against the devil's schemes. [12] For our struggle is not against flesh and blood, but against the rulers, against the authorities, against the powers of this dark world and against the spiritual forces of evil in the heavenly realms. [13] Therefore put on the full armor of God, so that when the day of evil comes, you may be able to stand your ground, and after you have done everything, to stand. [14] Stand firm then, with the belt of truth buckled around your waist, with the breastplate of righteousness in place, [15] and with your feet fitted with the readiness that comes from the gospel of peace. [16] In addition to all this, take up the shield of faith, with which you can extinguish all the flaming arrows of the evil one. [17] Take the helmet of salvation and the sword of the Spirit, which is the word of God. [18] And pray in the Spirit on all occasions with all kinds of prayers and requests. With this in mind, be alert and always keep on praying for all the Lord's people.

We must be like Elisha's servant, and have God open our eyes to see the hills full of horses and chariots of fire (2 Kings 6:17). Such passages are not fairy tales—they express reality. There are good angels with God who work for us (Hebrews 1:14), and there are evil angels with Satan who work against us. The battle is so fierce between these two forces that the great angel sent as a messenger to Daniel was detained for three weeks in Persia fighting against Satan's forces! Michael the archangel had to personally relieve him in the battle before he could come to Daniel (Daniel 10:1-3). Unquestionably, we are in a war, and it is past time to get into the fray wholeheartedly. The examples of warriors in the Old Testament should inspire us to run to the fight in the spiritual warfare before us.

I am inspired by Joshua and his army marching all night to do battle with the Amorites (Joshua 10). More inspiring is the fact that Joshua was so intent on destroying the enemy that he prayed for daylight to continue long enough to gain a total victory, and God gave him the extra day (verses 12-14). Joshua's battle instincts are also seen in his execution of the five captured kings after having his commanders place their feet on the kings' necks (verses 22-28). Joshua was not interested in compromising or allowing the enemy to have a place of refuge.

Some of us are probably a bit shocked by the apparent fierceness of these leaders. That reaction shows our problem in our battle with Satan. Had not Joshua done the job completely, these same enemies would have had to be fought again later. Until we get the intense desire to crucify our sinful natures (Galatians 5:24) and help others to do the same, our victories will always be short-lived! Too many of us are just plain wimpy when it comes to doing battle! Our American lifestyles have left us with weak, pampered characters instead of the strong, determined, fighting characters that God desires for us.

I am inspired by the old man Caleb who still wanted to fight those giants, the Anakites (Joshua 14:6-14). He felt as ready to do battle at 85 as he did at 40 years old, because he knew that God was the one who gave the victories. As Joshua 24:12-14 puts it: "I sent the hornet ahead of you, which drove them out before you—also the two Amorite kings. You did not do it with your own sword and bow. So I gave you a land on which you did not toil and cities you did not build; and you live in them and eat vineyards and olive groves that you did not plant. 'Now fear the Lord and serve him with all faithfulness." God still longs to send the hornet ahead of us, in order that we can conquer for Christ and spread the good news of the kingdom of God to the whole world. The conquest is yet before us. Are you ready to engage the enemy until death? If you have no cause worth dying for, you have no cause worth living for. Let's be bent on conquest!

QUESTIONS FOR THOUGHT

1. In what ways is Satan attacking you and what steps are you taking to prepare to defeat him?

2. Do you have a fierce determination to fight sin? Are you totally committed to "put to death...whatever belongs to your earthly nature" (Colossians 3:5)?

3. As you age, is your commitment to battle sin and evil growing or flaming out?

ACTION ITEMS

Gather your closest spiritual friends this week. Discuss Ephesians 6 and what putting on the full armor of God should involve. Inspect each other's armor and get a true assessment of whether each one of you is in the battle or not.

CHAPTER FOUR

Caleb: Give Me This Mountain!
Part 1

—Gordon Ferguson

"O God, from my youth you have taught me, and I still proclaim your wondrous deeds. So even to old age and grey hairs, O God, do not forsake me, until I proclaim your might to all the generations to come." (Psalms 71:17-19)

Caleb has long been a favorite of Bible readers because in his old age, he was still a warrior for God. When I was 79, I mentioned to my wife that we were old. She strongly disagreed (she is a year younger than me). But I then said that I was about to turn 80, to which she replied, "Well, 80 is old!" I believe old age attracts attention. When I was in my 60s and 70s, I was the brunt of many jokes about age. Now that I am in my 80s and definitely old, people must feel a bit sorry for me, for the age jokes have subsided! Thankfully, the Bible repeatedly says that old age is of great value. Some cultures understand this more than others, and for years I was blessed to teach in Asia where older people are highly respected. Older people, however, don't always set the right example spiritually. Some seasoned spiritual veterans will choose to sit back and let others do what they are more than qualified to do with their wealth of experience. That is not what I want my life to be about as I age; and thus far, it isn't by any stretch of the imagination.

The Bible provides us with great examples of those who were zealous for God in their golden years. I think of Paul, who never slowed down until the Roman officials removed his head. But my favorite old man is found in the Old Testament: Caleb, son of Jephunneh. Here is the passage that inspires me the most about him:

Joshua 14:10-13

[10] "Now then, just as the LORD promised, he has kept me alive for forty-five years since the time he said this to Moses, while Israel moved about in the wilderness. So here I am today, eighty-five years old! [11] I am still as strong today as the day Moses sent me out; I'm just as vigorous to go out to battle now as I was then. [12] Now give me this hill country that the LORD promised me that day. You yourself heard then that the Anakites were there and their cities were large and fortified, but, the LORD helping me, I will drive them out just as he said." [13] Then Joshua blessed Caleb son of Jephunneh and gave him Hebron as his inheritance.

While 85 might seem elderly to us, the life span during Caleb's day was longer, with some folks dying closer to 120 years of age. Yet, Caleb's example deserves the admiration he receives. Joshua 14:14 (and other passages), describe how Caleb was blessed because he followed the Lord "wholeheartedly." That is a lesson for the ages: God honors the ones who honor him. The aged man for the ages got it right in many ways when it came to following his God.

The Right Commitment

He began with having the right *commitment* by following God with his whole heart. So many people complain that God is not blessing them, but no one should expect to be blessed unless God has their whole heart. As the old saying goes, "either Jesus is Lord *of* all in our lives, or he is Lord not *at* all." He will never settle for second place. If you want to be blessed, imitate Caleb's commitment. Not only did he ultimately receive his mountain (or "hill country" in newer versions) because of this dedication, he followed God even when it wasn't popular. Joshua 14:6-9 describes how Caleb and Joshua stood against the rest of the leaders selected to originally spy out Canaan. He was not afraid of being different—to the point of being ridiculed.

The plague of being people-pleasers exerts pressure to conform on us all, young and old. But Jesus makes it plain that we are going against the crowd if we walk the narrow road that leads to eternal life with him (Matthew 7:13-14). A remarkable verse on how God views a committed heart is found in 2 Chronicles 16:9, which reads: "For the eyes of the LORD range throughout the earth to strengthen those whose hearts are fully committed to him." If we don't have that heart, things like complacency and materialism will consume us, because the heart cannot be fully dedicated to two things at once – something always wins the battle for first place.

As Jesus described this principle, he concluded with a rather startling statement: "No one can serve two masters. Either you will hate the one and love the other, or you will be devoted to the one and despise the other. You cannot serve both God and money" (Luke 16:13). Not much has changed since then, for materialism so easily becomes our master rather than Jesus. Caleb may have wanted his mountain badly, but he clearly was not divided in his heart between devotion to God and devotion to possessions.

The Right Ambition

Caleb also had the right *ambition.* He dreamed of possessing his mountain for 45 long years as the Israelites wandered in the desert. He had trodden on the land when sent out as one of the twelve to spy out the land (verse 9) and he never forgot the land nor Moses' promise to him about it. I remember so many of my ministry dreams, many of which came true, but some did not. The ones that didn't come true, I don't attribute to a lack of ambition or effort. God is still in charge. He sometimes closes one door to open another. At times, I even found myself rejoicing in what had initially disappointed me, for he did indeed open a better door. What kinds of spiritual dreams do you have? Dreams are what faith for the future is made of. Dreams for what you want your life to be, and the impact you want it to make on time and eternity are worthy dreams. Dreams for your family and friends, and what they can become and what impact their lives can make upon others are dreams of faith.

We all have dreams; the question is what kind of dreams they are. Some speak of their "dream job." How do you think God would define a dream job for you—money made, enjoyment, or impact on lives for eternity? Some speak of their "dream house." I have thankfully been blessed to live in many nice houses, but I too have a dream house—it's described in John 14:1-3! We can know where our hearts really are by the dreams that we have. And we can know what our dreams are by what we talk about and get most excited about. I know what excited Caleb: he wanted to conquer a mountain for God. I know what excited Jesus, because he spoke of it just before leaving earth—we call it the Great Commission. Jesus' disciples caught that dream from him and turned the world upside down. Do you have the right kinds of dreams like Caleb did, and the heart to go after them?

Part 2 will show us two other qualities that enabled God to bless Caleb with his dream of climbing and conquering a mountain for his God. Keep reading (but only after answering the questions and planning your action items)!

QUESTIONS FOR THOUGHT

1. When you looked at the passages about spiritual commitment, how did you feel about your own level of commitment? Explain.

2. What are ways in which spiritual ambition or dreams can be wrong and misguided? What are ways in which they are right and needed?

3. How has aging affected you emotionally and spiritually?

ACTION ITEMS

Make a list of the qualities, attitudes and actions that you see in Caleb that you want to imitate, and list one action that you are going to act upon this week.

CHAPTER FIVE

Caleb: Give Me This Mountain!
Part 2

—Gordon Ferguson

"Therefore I tell you, whatever you ask for in prayer, believe
that you have received it, and it will be yours." (Mark 11:24)

In Part 1 of our study of Caleb, we saw that Caleb was blessed by getting things right in his heart and life. We looked at his wholehearted commitment to God and his driving ambition which kept his dream alive for 45 years. As the story continues, we will discover two more qualities that led ultimately to him receiving the right reward. We will begin with his unceasing prayer.

The Right Prayer Request

Yes, Caleb had the right prayer—he asked for it (Joshua 14:12). The Bible says a lot about asking in prayer, but we can make either good or bad requests.

James 4:2-3

[2] "You want something but don't get it. You kill and covet, but you cannot have what you want. You quarrel and fight. You do not have, because you do not ask God. [3] When you ask, you do not receive, because you ask with wrong motives, that you may spend what you get on your pleasures."

Mark 11:24

[24] "Therefore I tell you, whatever you ask for in prayer, believe that you have received it, and it will be yours."

Prayer is one thing in my life that I could not survive without. I started learning to pray in earnest when I was approaching forty years old and experiencing some sort of a midlife crisis. I was desperate and began walking and praying out loud. I can pray just fine on my knees with other people, but when praying this way alone, my mind wanders too much. Walking and praying aloud keeps me focused. In all the places we have lived since that time in my life, and there have been many, I always find some solitary places to be alone and pray. I have names for some of my favorite ones. I have fought many spiritual battles in those places, and I often think back through them and thank God for them.

For many decades, I have started my days with prayer times, often when out in nature. In the past several years, I do my best praying when journaling. As a writer, I think through my fingers as my heart comes out. With either approach, I simply have to unburden my soul to start each day. Some of my best prayer times are when I just spend time thanking God, going through my life, and remembering all my blessings. I especially love doing it on or around Thanksgiving. I also ask God to bless what I do for the good of others; to bless my family and the church family; and many individuals by name—I believe all of that is extremely important to the life of every believer.

I have a long prayer list with people on it who are facing trials of all types. I started that list many years ago because I knew that a day would come when I would want others to put me on their prayer list as I faced a crisis, and that day came in 2022. The prayers of many brothers and sisters in Christ all over the world pulled me through a near death experience, and that experience brought unexpected blessings into my life. I had a book published recently (2024) about that experience entitled, *My Roller Coaster Ride With God and Cancer.* I thank God daily for those prayer warriors whose prayers for me were answered—with a yes!

The Right Courage

Further, Caleb had the right *courage*—he was not afraid of obstacles. His age could have been one of those obstacles, but in Joshua 14:10-11, he amazingly said: "So here I am today, 85 years old! I am still as strong today as the day Moses sent me out; I'm just as vigorous to go out to battle now as I was then." It was the same strength because it was God's strength, and 45 years could not change that! I remember a comment by an elder years ago about turning things over to the younger members and taking a back seat. No one among us needs to take a back seat, young or old, because God delights in working in us and through us to accomplish his purposes on this earth. We do need to provide the younger ones among us the opportunities to develop their leadership skills, but we are never too young or too old to be used mightily by God to make a difference in this world for him.

Giants in the land were another potential obstacle. In Joshua 14:12, they were called the Anakites. When the twelve spied out the land forty years earlier, they had seen these giants, but had two different reactions.

Numbers 13:30-33

[30] Then Caleb silenced the people before Moses and said, "We should go up and take possession of the land, for we can certainly do it." [31] But the men who had gone up with him said, "We can't attack those people; they are stronger than we are." [32] And they spread among the Israelites a bad report about the land they had explored. They said, "The land we explored devours those living in it. All the people we saw there are of great size. [33] We saw the Nephilim there (the descendants of Anak come from the Nephilim). We seemed like grasshoppers in our own eyes, and we looked the same to them."

A very important principle is found in that statement: "We seemed like grasshoppers in our own eyes." Many of us fall prey to that type of self-defeating thinking. We have our own "giants" to conquer, the ones that exist in our own minds and which keep us from being all for God that he created us to be. Fear should not block what God intends to do with us, for the answer is in him, not in ourselves. God has given us too many promises to miss the point that we are sons and daughters of the King, and our confidence should be in him and his power to accomplish his purposes.

Ephesians 3:20

"Now to him who is able to do immeasurably more than all we ask or imagine, according to his power that is at work within us."

Philippians 4:13
"I can do all things through Christ who gives me strength."

When we, like Caleb, have the right commitment, ambition, prayer and courage, the right reward is guaranteed. Old Caleb received his mountain. When the smoke of battle had cleared away and the last clash of swords had been heard, it was the giants who had fallen, while God's octogenarian stood strong! We have the same God today, and in the stirring words of Romans 8:31, "What, then, shall we say in response to these things? If God is for us, who can be against us?" Who indeed!

I love the example of Caleb, the old man with a young man's heart. With him, age was inconsequential; what mattered most was his heart toward God. When our history is written about our lives, how will it read? The answer to that one is in our hearts for God right now. Where are we and where do we want to be? What decisions will we make today to help us get there? All we have is today. Let's make it count for time and eternity!

QUESTIONS FOR THOUGHT

1. How would you describe your prayer life in the past six months, and how do you feel about it?

2. How do courage and fear fit together in your thinking? What are ways that fears hold you back in areas that are important to you?

3. In looking at both parts of this study of Caleb, what were the top two or three things that convicted you about needing to change in your own life?

ACTION ITEMS

In response to question #3 above, write an action plan to make at least two changes in your life and then share them with friends, asking them to ask you weekly for a month about how you are doing in putting these things into practice.

CHAPTER SIX

The Samaritan Women

—Theresa Ferguson

The story of the Samaritan woman in John 4 is remarkable from a number of vantage points. For a Jew to even engage in conversation with a "half-breed" Samaritan would be considered by fellow Jews not simply as unusual, but unsavory. For a Jewish man, and one recognized by the people as a Rabbi at that, to speak to a Samaritan woman in broad daylight just wouldn't be done—unless you were God in the flesh, of course. There's more: Jesus designates her as the first person other than those in his inner circle to be told that he was the Messiah. He also sends her happily away as the first one to share the gospel story outside the confines of Judaism. This historic and dramatic interaction was far more remarkable than we in our modern Western setting can imagine.

From our modern vantage point, we get hung up thinking of how immoral she must have been, having been married five times and shacked up with someone to whom she was not married. We cannot accurately fathom all the dynamics involved, given the fact that women in that culture were dependent on men for support. Businesswomen like Lydia (Acts 16) and Phoebe (Romans 16) were few and far between; and unlike the Samaritan woman, they were Jews with networking possibilities all over the world. Samaritans were not privileged with such. But whatever was true of this woman of Samaria in the moral realm, the fact remains that Jesus selected her to do something unique at that stage of his ministry. As always, God in the Spirit or in the flesh is unpredictable!

The Impact of Love on a Heart

What must have gone on inside this woman's heart to be treated as special rather than as an outcast! In another passage, the

Apostle John made a statement that fits this story quite well: "We love because he first loved us" (1 John 4:19). Jesus' encounter with the Samaritan woman provides us with a wonderful example of what God's love does to radically change our hearts. This woman felt God's love in a way that compelled her to go back to her village and tell everyone about Jesus. How could she not?

My favorite romantic movies usually involve someone reluctant to offer their hearts until the one pursuing their affections taps into a need they didn't know they had. Jesus won over the Samaritan woman in a similar way. She only had her sights set on getting water, a process interrupted by what must have been an unsettling incidence of a Jewish male being present. God moves in mysterious ways his wonders to perform, as the old hymn puts it. Just why Jesus took this journey to the North we don't know, but with him nothing was ever a matter of coincidence. Chronologically in John's Gospel, he had recently cleared out the temple courts, so the aftermath of that event might have inspired his trip, but we know one of them now from the events recorded in John 4. All the events of your life which seemed incidental at the time may not have been, whether we saw the significance in them or not.

Jesus initiated the conversation with this anxious woman with a very simple request: asking for a drink of water. But from her vantage point, there was nothing simple about that request. Social codes were being smashed. In verses 10-15, Jesus offered her living water. She didn't understand what that meant yet, but now her guard was down, and she became comfortable asking a number of questions. Jesus had just told her that he was the Messiah when the apostles returned from their trip for food. She undoubtedly understood the significance of Jesus' self-disclosure as she hastily left her water jar behind to hurry home and spread the good news. She also left her bewilderment behind as well (perhaps passing it on to the apostles who were trying to process the unfolding drama). I suspect she also left behind most of her painful past.

Leaving Behind the Past—and the Present

When our sins (as they are biblically defined) are made obvious, we become anxious to leave our pasts behind. I am sure the Samaritan woman experienced this. The real challenge comes when we are asked to give up the parts of our "present" that we value. I doubt she had much in her present life that was of value. She might have just been in survival mode. Life for most in that setting and for untold numbers in our day is terribly difficult. But those of us in the Western world, particularly in the United States, may be blessed with material possessions and other things that have a hold on us emotionally. How willing are we to give them up? Someone has said that spiritual sacrifice often involves giving up something good for something better. If we intend to follow Jesus on his terms, we had best get comfortable with that definition, as the following passage explains:

Luke 9:23-24

[23] Then he said to them all: "Whoever wants to be my disciple must deny themselves and take up their cross daily and follow me. [24] For whoever wants to save their life will lose it, but whoever loses their life for me will save it.

What did this woman at the well "lose" for Jesus? Everything, for now all that mattered was telling others about her newfound Messiah. As the rest of the story indicates, her focus was singular, and its results were profound. She adopted the focus of Jesus, who came to seek and save the lost (Luke 19:10). As the returning disciples urged Jesus to eat something, he replied, "I have food to eat that you know nothing about," which he described as doing the will of God and accomplishing his work (John 4:31-34). From there, he immediately began talking about the fields being ripe for harvest. He was so consumed with the idea of saving people that he lost his appetite for physical food. Spiritual food had taken its place.

At the request of the Samaritans who had believed because of the woman's testimony, Jesus stayed two days to minister to those who were now hungering and thirsting for righteousness in the person of Jesus. It would have been quite interesting to know how long it took the apostles to get over their shock and accept the obvious, that salvation was not going to have the limitations that Judaism had. Although it would take years for the gospel to officially be taken to all parts of the world for all races of people, it would seem certain that this evangelistic foray into Samaria would have remained in the memory of the apostles. No one would be off limits for the gospel message, for it was a message of salvation for *all.*

Acts 1:8 contained Jesus' plan for spreading the gospel, and Samaria was the logical place after Judea. Acts 8 describes how the gospel spread to Samaria through Philip's preaching. Crowds came out to hear Philip preach in great numbers, no doubt influenced by the foundation laid in John 4. An enchanting encounter with a very unlikely woman led to an unprecedented result that no one could have imagined. The Samaritan woman loved because Jesus first loved her, and from that point, her life took on a whole new meaning and direction. His love left her with his purpose. Has his love left you with the same purpose? Does your life demonstrate it? When I think of the effect of Jesus' encounter with this woman and how it left her feeling, I think of Psalm 18:35: "You make your saving help my shield, and your right hand sustains me; your help has made me great."

QUESTIONS FOR THOUGHT

1. How has Jesus' impact changed your life in terms of having a hunger to share the good news with others?

2. Do you tend to overestimate your value to Jesus and his purposes, or do you tend to underestimate them? What lessons can you learn from the Samaritan woman's example?

3. The apostles would have overlooked the value of this woman because of her ethnicity and her background. Which types of people do you tend to overlook?

ACTION ITEMS

If "the work of God" in the mind of Jesus was to focus on a spiritual harvest of souls, make your own plan to pray, and maybe fast, to develop a similar hunger. Write down some goals for your personal evangelism. Imitate the Samaritan woman!

CHAPTER SEVEN

Deborah the Judge, Judges 4:1-5:31 Part 1

—Theresa Ferguson

The people who witnessed the conquest under Joshua remained faithful to God. But for whatever reason, they did not instill that faithfulness in the hearts of their children. Judges 2:10 gives us the sad report that "after that whole generation had been gathered to their fathers, another generation grew up, who knew neither the Lord nor what he had done for Israel." (Read Judges 2:6-23.) The people fell headlong into idol worship, prostituting themselves with Baal and Ashtaroth and breaking the heart of their faithful God.

Each time God allowed their rebellion to cause them to be sold into slavery to surrounding nations, they cried out for deliverance—bowing once again to the one true God who could save them. Each time his own gracious nature prompted God to raise up a leader who would deliver his people from the clutches of their enemies. As long as this leader, or judge, was alive, they continued to bring victory to the people. Unfortunately, after the death of each judge, the people would slide back into the mire of idolatry. This deadly cycle repeated itself time after time during the entire period of the Judges. Judges 17:6 describes this period succinctly: "In those days Israel had no king; everyone did as they saw fit." Other versions say that everyone did what was "right in their own eyes." This type of neglect of God's will bring calamity on any nation, past or present.

The God-given structure of Israel's loose government called for a male leader. Mostly, women played important, but back-seat roles in the affairs of the nation. But on one especially rare occasion, God did the extra-ordinary. He did the unpredictable. He raised up a woman to lead his people. She was made to shine as a ray of hope in a time of dark despair. Her name was Deborah. Only two people in the Old Testament were said to be both prophet and judge: Deborah and Samuel. Impressive company to be sure!

We first meet Deborah sitting under the Palm of Deborah judging disputes between her people. She was unlike the other judges who were all males and usually military leaders. Deborah was the only female judge. Besides this amazing exaltation, she was also a prophetess—a spokesperson for God himself. Just how this woman ascended to the lofty position of being a judge and a prophetess in Israel, we are not told. Why God would break his normal order of things to exalt a woman to not only a high position, but a position held only by men both before and after her, we are not told. Surely this woman was a woman among women—a standout in every sense of the word.

What we do know about this remarkable leader is that she was the wife of an otherwise unknown man, Lappidoth, and that she lived in the hill country of Ephraim. We also know she exhibited great *faithfulness* before God at a time when most of her countrymen were overwhelmed with great f*earfulness*! Her exceptional personal qualities would fill a long list. She was *bold* enough to call the top male military leader to come to her *and* challenge him to lead the Israelite army into battle with the enemy nation of Canaan. She expected him to do what she asked, for she had the confidence that she was giving the very orders of God. She was *humble* enough to let Barak, her fearful counterpart, do the actual leading of the army despite his initial reluctance. She was brave enough to personally lure Sisera, the opposing army commander, into battle and then to go into the battle herself (an unheard-of feat for a woman of that day)!

Walking by Faith, Not by Sight

Perhaps her most outstanding quality, however, was the unquestioning *faith* she had in God at a time when little evidence could be produced that God was really with the nation. In fact, for 20 years God had not delivered them from the hands of their enemies. Can you imagine what 20 years of oppression would do to the faith of ordinary people? Most of us can muster some faith when there is at least some evidence of God working in our lives. We can take a good situation and develop faith to make it better. But the ability to look at defeat after defeat while maintaining faith is a staggering proposition indeed. This woman Deborah looked at the circumstances of repeated defeat yet expected victory anyway. *Amazing!* She trusted the words of God, and not her own evaluation of her situation. Nor was she influenced negatively by the faithlessness of everyone around her, including Barak. She didn't simply *face* the facts—she *faithed* the facts!

When Barak followed the instructions of Deborah and gathered an army, Sisera responded by gathering his army, which included 900 iron chariots. This woman of faith was not shaken in the least but "loaned" her faith to Barak with these final challenging words: "Go! This is the day the LORD has given Sisera into your hands. Has not the LORD gone ahead of you (Judges 4:14)?" When great faith coupled with obedience exists in people, God gives a great victory. The description of this victory is recorded in Judges 4:15-16 with these heart-stirring words: "At Barak's advance, the LORD routed Sisera and all his chariots and army by the sword, and Sisera abandoned his chariot and fled on foot. But Barak pursued the chariots and army as far as Harosheth Haggoyim. All the troops of Sisera fell by the sword; not a man was left."

A Lesser Hero but a Hero Still

The stars of this show were two women, Deborah and Jael; yet Barak was also a hero. This passage is sometimes used to suggest that Barak was a total coward, but a closer examination of the passage would suggest otherwise. What exactly does Judges 4–5 say about him? First, he was directly chosen by God, according to the prophetess, Deborah. Second, he was smart enough to ask the leader of Israel, a prophetess and judge, to accompany him. He most likely wanted assurance that what Deborah said was truly commanded by God, which her willingness to enter the battle with him would have proven. Third, he led the Israelite army into the battle, although clearly outmanned. Fourth, once the opposing army started retreating, posing no other immediate threat, he still pursued them until every last man was killed. Fifth, he wasn't threatened by women leadership. In fact, he both sought it and praised it. His and Deborah's prophetic song in Judges 5 included high praise for Jael, the other female hero. Finally, let's not forget that Barak is found in the list of Old Testament heroes in Hebrews 11. "And what more shall I say? I do not have time to tell about Gideon, Barak, Samson and Jephthah, about David and Samuel and the prophets (Hebrews 11:32)."

QUESTIONS FOR THOUGHT

1. Do you believe that most Bible believers are aware of the influence of women leaders in both the Old and New Testaments? Explain your answer.

2. What parallels do you see between the period of the Judges and America?

3. How does the faith of Deborah show up most vividly? List all the ways you see in the passage.

ACTION ITEMS

Barak was influenced by Deborah to engage in a battle that carried significant risks. Think of three people whom you could encourage to put their faith into action in areas where fears are holding them back, and then encourage them to act.

CHAPTER EIGHT

Deborah the Judge, Judges 4:1-5:31 Part 2

—Theresa Ferguson

In Part 1 of Deborah's story, we were introduced to her as a person and as an outstanding leader. In fact, in the Old Testament, she was a unique leader as a female. She and Samuel were the only two people in the Old Testament designated as both prophet and judge. As we will note a bit later, women leaders were much more prominent in the Old Testament than often assumed. That said, this story of two victorious women is quite unique. We have met Deborah, and now let's meet Jael with her nail!

Hitting the Nail on the Head!

From a woman's perspective, the most exciting part of the battle was yet to come! The sole survivor of the battle mentioned in Part 1 was the commander, Sisera. He fled on foot to the tent of Jael, the wife of Heber the Kennite, who in the past had been on friendly terms with Sisera's king. Whether Heber may have been favorable toward Sisera or not, we do not know. What we do know is that Deborah's example had evidently inspired a nation of women to step outside their household duties and put their hands to the battle. At least that was the case with one of those women, Jael. She boldly greeted Sisera and cleverly fed him warm milk, which acted as a sedative to this war-weary commander. When he fell into a deep sleep, Jael took a nail, deftly hit the nail on (and into) Sisera's head, and the rest is history. As Deborah had said, the honor for the victory did indeed go to a woman. Barak saw the fulfillment when he came to the tent of this new national heroine and was shown the dead commander. Barak was the third person on the scale of heroes that day, and the two before him were both *women!*

After the victory, the humility of Deborah was seen in the way that she shared the victory with Barak. As a woman leader of great influence, she was strong but supportive of the male leader in the nation. She was in no way insecure or competitive with him. Whether she was in front leading or in the rear encouraging, she was secure in who she was and in what she was trying to accomplish for her God. Seeking success for God is a very different thing than seeking success for oneself. The beautiful song of victory in Judges 5 was not a *solo* by Deborah, but a *duet* with Barak, with whom she shared the celebration. The focus of Deborah's heart was on glorifying God rather than seeking recognition for herself or for Barak. Her marvelous love for God and for her people is expressed wonderfully in these well-known words which begin the song (5:2): "When the princes in Israel take the lead, when the people willingly offer themselves—praise the LORD!"

Female Leadership is of God

It has been observed, accurately, that female leadership in the Old Testament is often hidden in plain sight. Certainly, Deborah's and Jael's exploits have not been hidden, yet others have definitely been overlooked. Let's list a few. To start, the first four prophets listed in Genesis include a woman. They are, in order of mention, Abraham, Aaron, Miriam and Moses. In Micah 6:4, God recounts bringing Israel out of Egypt, stating, "I sent Moses to lead you, also Aaron and Miriam." Second, in 2 Chronicles 34, we read about another female prophet, Huldah. King Josiah went to her for very important advice about the recently discovered copy of the Law of Moses. Other prophets were available, including Jeremiah, but he showed his confidence in the female prophet. Interesting! Third, Queen Esther saved her fellow Jews in Persia and instituted the Feast of Purim, an added official Jewish feast of which God himself approved. Female leadership in the New Testament is in no way hidden, for the first gospel sermon by Peter in Acts 2 foretold that women prophets were going to be an ordinary, functional part of Christ's kingdom (verses 17-18).

Faithful Not Fearful

Fearful! Mistrustful! Afraid of rejection! Afraid to tell anyone who I really was inside! Afraid to let the emotional wall down! Most of my early life I was controlled by the sins which I had allowed Satan to sow deeply into my heart. Like the Israelites in the days of Deborah, I also felt oppressed. But thank God I listened to his word and obeyed it so I could be liberated from those crippling sins. I am so thankful to God for women like Deborah who have inspired me to overcome numerous challenges in my life as if they were among my closest friends.

The causes of my mistrust began with having an alcoholic father whose frequent violent actions and rejection set fear into my heart. Through the years, I became increasingly mistrustful of even religious people, especially leaders, because of some bad experiences in the denominational world. To top it off, my husband, a preacher in one of these denominational groups, was often harsh and insensitive toward my feelings. (Thankfully, he became a disciple and has changed dramatically.) Finally, once I became a true disciple, God began to lead me to victory over these fears and mistrust. Praise God!

It takes a daily commitment to stay victorious over fearfulness and related sins. Like Deborah, I must keep listening to God daily about who I am: a woman chosen by God to speak his words to others. Satan attacks my heart daily to fan my fears into flame, attempting to stop me from carrying out the plans that God has for my life. When I really listen to the great promises of the Lord, my faith always overpowers my tendency to fear. As in Judges 5, when Deborah recited the tremendous victories which God had given the Israelites, I must recite the victories which God has given to me and to those other faithful warriors around me.

On a very practical basis, when the fear demon really goes after me, I have to expose the temptations very blatantly. I list all the fear temptations on a sheet of paper and cry out to God to rebuke the demon of fear in the name of Jesus. One by one, I surrender each fear temptation to him completely, after which I tear up the paper. Then I write out appropriate promises from God's word which I hold on to as a weapon against Satan for the rest of the day. I expect success, thanking God in advance for the victory which I then claim by faith. It is very important to go out quickly and do the very thing that has been producing the fear in me. This approach, as simple as it may seem at first glance, has helped many other women who have come to me for help to deal with all sorts of fears.

As Deborah was filled with gratitude for the victory given by God, I can never thank God enough for the numerous victories he has given me. At age 81, I look back at the past decades and marvel at the wonderful marriage I now have with my precious partner in the gospel, my children and grandchildren, and the opportunity to live out the answer to the last prayer that Deborah prayed to God: "May they who love you be like the sun when it rises in its strength (Judges 5:32)."

QUESTIONS FOR THOUGHT

1. On a scale of 1-10, how would you rate your average level of mistrust? How about your average level of fear?

2. What are some ways you can "faith the facts" behind your mistrust and fears?

3. In studying the story of Deborah, Jael and Barak, list and describe the strengths of each.

ACTION ITEMS

Follow the instructions in the next-to-last paragraph regarding how to successfully deal with your "fear demons." Don't leave any of the steps out that are mentioned. This is a powerful tool to help you overcome the fear that can stifle your faith.

SECTION TWO

Victorious Christian Living

[13] *"You are the salt of the earth. But if the salt loses its saltiness, how can it be made salty again? It is no longer good for anything, except to be thrown out and trampled underfoot.*

[14] *"You are the light of the world. A town built on a hill cannot be hidden.* [15] *Neither do people light a lamp and put it under a bowl. Instead they put it on its stand, and it gives light to everyone in the house.* [16] *In the same way, let your light shine before others, that they may see your good deeds and glorify your Father in heaven.*

—Matthew 5:13-16

The Message of the Cross

—Theresa Ferguson with Linda Brumley

"For the message of the cross is foolishness to those who are perishing, but to us who are being saved it is the power of God." (1 Corinthians 1:18)

The message of the cross cannot be explained or analyzed in words of human wisdom. It is through the cross that we come to know the unknowable love of God (Ephesians 3:16-19). The cross displays his grace, mercy, compassion, justice, unchallenged others-centeredness, and the extent of his desire and ability to forgive the unforgivable. It is this compelling love that motivates a new lifestyle. "Follow God's example, therefore, as dearly loved children and walk in the way of love, just as Christ loved us and gave himself up for us as a fragrant offering and sacrifice to God" (Ephesians 5:1-2). The cross is our motivation to sacrifice, submit, love, suffer, serve, and teach. The cross is our power, our purpose, and our victory. It provides us with the highest motivation possible in each of the following areas.

Motivation to Sacrifice

No opportunity for giving (whether of money, time, energy, or life) could present itself in a way that would allow us to argue that it was "too much to ask." A God who has given his very best and his all when we were utterly unworthy is fully worthy of asking for our best. Paul said, "Therefore, I urge you, brothers and sisters, in view of God's mercy, to offer your bodies as a living sacrifice, holy and pleasing to God—this is your true and proper worship" (Romans 12:1-2).

Motivation to Submit

Setting aside my will for the will of God or another person is a difficult test. My will is strong. But if my Lord was able to set aside his will in Gethsemane to submit to my needs on Calvary, I want to be like him. I want to learn to reverently submit like he did (Hebrews 5:7-8).

Motivation to Love

Because God fully expressed his heart for me on the cross, I want to have his heart for others. I want to love as unselfishly and unconditionally and constantly as he does. Those I once considered unlovable, I no longer regard from a worldly point of view (2 Corinthians 5:11-21).

Motivation to Suffer

Trials are opportunities to become more like Jesus. When being like him is our highest goal, trials are a joy (Luke 6:22-23). However, if we value comfort more than Christlikeness, trials will be agony (Philippians 3:10; 1 Peter 2:21-25).

Motivation to Serve

Jesus paid my debt of sin and now I owe a debt of love. The cross declares that no amount of humble, sacrificial service is beyond our call of duty (Luke 17:7-10). We never need to evaluate whether someone deserves our service. Jesus asked us to serve others and he deserves it (Matthew 15:31-46)!

Motivation to Teach

Because we have been saved by the cross, we hold out the cross to others. At last, a purpose in life greater than self! "All this is from God, who reconciled us to himself through Christ and gave us the ministry of reconciliation" (2 Corinthians 5:18). No other focus in life apart from the cross will motivate this kind of lifestyle. Without the cross, our work for God will be a burdensome duty. We will burn out; we will lose our first love. The cross is our entrance into the kingdom of God through baptism. It is our weekly celebration of victory in the Lord's supper. It provides our daily access to the presence of God and the power of the Holy Spirit.

Our Power

The message of the cross is the power of God to save everyone who believes (Romans 1:16-17). The cross is the crux of God's message and must be the heart of our message as well. This power of God provides the force, strength, and authority behind our teaching. Therefore, we are not ashamed of the message of the cross and its power because of its effect in our lives.

Power to Draw

The cross contains the power to draw us to God (John 12:32). The fact that Christ emptied himself, became the humblest of men, and died as a criminal for each of us personally, draws us like a magnet. His example gives us the power to likewise deny ourselves, take up our cross, and follow him.

Power to Save

The message of the cross has the power to save us (Romans 5:6-10). When we were totally without power, the sinless died for the sinner because of his amazing love for us. He took our place on the cross in order that we might take his place in the world and do even greater things than he did (John 14:12).

Power to Transform

The gospel of God's grace can transform us into his image (2 Corinthians 3:18). At baptism we are transformed out of darkness into light. As a Christian, we are transformed daily by the renewing of our minds (Romans 12:2). Therefore, from the beginning to the end, our spiritual lives are a direct result of the power of the cross.

Our Purpose

The cross becomes our purpose in life. Jesus' reason for dying (to save mankind) is our reason for living. With the same compassion that would prompt us to offer ourselves as guides to the physically blind, we offer ourselves as guides to the spiritually blind to help "open their eyes." We want them to see that the cross is neither a stumbling block nor foolishness, but the power and wisdom of God (1 Corinthians 1:18-24). Paul explains Satan's role in spiritual blindness in 2 Corinthians 4:4, "The god of this age has blinded the minds of unbelievers, so that they cannot see the light of the gospel of the glory of Christ, who is the image of God." What a joy to defeat Satan by giving sight to the blind!

Our Victory

The cross provides our victory over sin, guilt, and ultimate damnation. Without question, Satan has been defeated. This victory is ours if we claim it. But we need to see our conquest with an expansive view. Biblically, salvation is described as past, present, and future. Through the cross, we have been saved by grace through faith (Ephesians 2:8). Timothy was reminded of the time when he had made the good confession in the sight of many witnesses (1 Timothy 6:12). We can look back to our baptism into Christ and know that we won a victory over sin. Salvation is also a present reality, as we are in the process of being saved (1 Corinthians 1:18). When we are consistently walking in God's light, the blood of Christ continually cleanses us from all sin (1 John 1:5-9). Victorious living is an everyday reality in Christ. Our ultimate victory is to enter heaven itself. In this sense, salvation is nearer than when we first believed (Romans 13:11). It is yet future. But the indwelling Spirit is our guarantee that we shall inherit what is to come (2 Corinthians 1:21-22). Praise God for our victory—past, present, and future!

QUESTIONS FOR THOUGHT

1. As you think about your walk with God, what are the motivations that keep you inspired for God?

2. How often do you study about the cross and the sacrifice of Christ? Are you using it to empower your faith? Does it help you to make every effort?

3. Do you see your life as victorious or are you burdened by sins and the oppression of the world. How can the cross motivate you to overcome the obstacles of life and the world?

ACTION ITEMS

Take time this week to read the crucifixion accounts in the gospels. Let them motivate you to grow and impact the world (Matthew 26-28; Mark 14-16; Luke 22-24; John 17-20).

CHAPTER TEN

Living Sacrifices: Motivation and Definition, Part 1

—Gordon Ferguson

"Therefore, I urge you, brothers and sisters, in view of God's mercy, to offer your bodies as a living sacrifice, holy and pleasing to God—this is your true and proper worship. 2 Do not conform to the pattern of this world, but be transformed by the renewing of your mind. Then you will be able to test and approve what God's will is—his good, pleasing and perfect will." (Romans 12:1-2)

In the first two verses of Romans 12, Paul teaches powerful lessons about our need to be living sacrifices. Verse one describes the *motivation* to sacrifice and the *definition* of the sacrifice, while verse two explains the *process* of sacrificial living and the *results* of it. Therefore, part one of this two-part series will cover verse one, and part two will cover the second verse.

The Motivation

The *motivation* to offer ourselves to God as living sacrifices is twofold—the human and the divine. Paul was urging the believers to follow through with the commitment they made when they decided to make Jesus the Lord of their lives. The call is always to be totally surrendered to Christ and his kingdom. Baptism into Christ must be predicated on such surrender, and the continuing walk with him will sustain this commitment. But in order to keep this devotion as our top priority, we must stay yoked with Jesus to make our burdens light and have fellow believers urging us along.

Paul gave such an admonition in a general sense, but he knew that the specific human motivation was a matter of discipleship. Romans, along with all his other writings, clearly laid out our "one another responsibilities." Without people in our lives helping us to mature, we will never become what we were designed to be. The missing ingredient in religion generally is the ingredient of discipleship, and yet it is at the very center of the Great Commission in Matthew 28:18-20. Praise God he has called us back to this most basic element of Christianity which allows us to radically change, and to then radically change the world!

The divine side of our needed motivation is *gratitude* for God's mercy. The word translated "mercy" is plural in the original language—the *mercies* of God. His grace is so varied that the most eloquent speaker or most gifted writer can only give us an introductory insight into it. God *delights* in showing mercy and granting forgiveness. His forgiveness is described in both Old and New Testaments in the most picturesque terms possible. He wants us to be assured that he is always the God of the new beginning, not just at baptism, but afterwards at the precise time we request that new beginning with a disciple's heart! Actually, if we are walking in the light, forgiveness is continual, as 1 John 1:5-7 shows, but we still need to ask for it to both keep our own consciences completely clear and our hearts humble (1 John 1:8-10). Because of his mercy, shown in forgiveness, the past has no power to drag us down.

The Definition

The *definition* of this living sacrifice is also seen in Romans 12:1. **First,** a sacrifice of our *bodies.* Believing the correct things is important but doing them is more important. What we do with our bodies demonstrates whether we are slaves to sin (Satan) or slaves to righteousness (God). "Don't you know that when you offer yourselves to someone as obedient slaves, you are slaves of the one you obey—whether you are slaves to sin, which leads to death, or to obedience, which leads to righteousness?" (Romans 6:16). If we are to be Christ's slaves, it takes determination and discipline. Paul made that clear to the Corinthian disciples when he said, "No, I strike a blow to my body and make it my slave so

that after I have preached to others, I myself will not be disquali-
fied for the prize" (1 Corinthians 9:27).

Second, our sacrifice is a *living one.* It is not the sacrifice of
better days in the past, but a daily walk with God. It is living—in
the sense of growing and changing—rather than keeping the status
quo. Anything which is not growing is dying. Personal growth
is not easy. When farming, cultivating, planting, watering, and
weeding are necessary parts of the process. It is only when we do
not grow weary that we harvest the crop (Galatians 6:7-9). Without consistent attention to growth, we will ultimately die before
harvest. And God wants *living sacrifices,* not dead ones!

Third, our sacrifice is to be *holy.* The consistent challenge
of God is to be holy as he is holy. Animal sacrifices in the Old
Testament were to be holy and without blemish. Our lives before
God are to be righteous and blameless. Being blameless is not
perfection, but consistent faithfulness. It is walking in the light,
being open about our sin, and being cleansed by his blood (1 John
1:7-9). It is a determination to be holy at all costs, which always
allows us to flourish and grow in the fruit of the Spirit.

Fourth, the *sacrifice* of our lives is to be pleasing to God.
Therefore, our sacrifice must be aligned with what we read in his
word. Reading and studying the Bible can never be neglected. No
human will ever know everything in the Word, but we must *want*
to know God intimately and be empowered by his presence in and
his desires for our lives. Since we are going to be judged by the
revealed word of God (John 12:48; James 2:12), we must seek to
understand and apply it. If we stay pleasing to him now, we will
be later when we must give an account!

Fifth, our sacrifice is *spiritual worship.* The world's concept
of worship is limited to a few activities at a set time and place.
God's concept is that we worship in all that we do in every situation. Colossians 3:17 makes this abundantly clear. "And whatever
you do, whether in word or deed, do it all in the name of the Lord
Jesus, giving thanks to God the Father through him." Worship is
more about what we *are* than what we *do.* Church assemblies are
not to be the only time we worship as some may think. We do
not assemble to worship as individuals; we assemble to worship

together as God's family. Worship as Paul describes it in this passage is a continual sacrifice of our hearts and lives before God, all day every day. In view of these truths, what kind of worshipper are you? What kind of sacrifice is your life?

QUESTIONS FOR THOUGHT

1. Discipleship has both a vertical aspect (us and Christ) and a horizontal aspect (the "one another" relationships with other disciples). How would you rate yourself in these two aspects and why?

2. Do you believe you are capable of consistently keeping your vertical discipleship strong with Christ without having people in your life to encourage you and motivate you? Explain why or why not?

3. Give thought to this statement about worship, how you understand it and how well you are practicing it. "We do not assemble to worship; we assemble to worship *together;* our worship is a continual sacrifice of our hearts and lives before God."

ACTION ITEMS

Consider the *motivation* and *definition* of being a living sacrifice and list two or three things that you need to improve in. Make a plan for putting them into practice and act upon each of them this week. Each journey begins with a small step. Start walking.

CHAPTER ELEVEN

Living Sacrifices: Process and Results, Part 2

—Gordon Ferguson

"Therefore, I urge you, brothers and sisters, in view of God's mercy, to offer your bodies as a living sacrifice, holy and pleasing to God—this is your true and proper worship. 2 Do not conform to the pattern of this world, but be transformed by the renewing of your mind. Then you will be able to test and approve what God's will is—his good, pleasing and perfect will." (Romans 12:1-2)

Part 1 of this two-part series discussed the *motivation* to sacrifice and the *definition* of sacrifice, as presented in Romans 12:1. This second part centers around verse 2 as it relates to the *process* of sacrifice and the *results* of sacrificial living.

The Process

The process of sacrifice includes a rejection of sin (a refusal to conform to the world); and an acceptance of righteousness (a decision to be transformed by the renewing of our minds). Traditional religion has always emphasized the former while neglecting the latter. The results have been appalling. People have tried excluding the evil without totally committing to Jesus' way of living. In fact, becoming like Jesus is the means to keeping Satan out. Colossians 3 describes the process as "taking off" and "putting on." The person described in Matthew 12 who cleaned out his life of demons and left his house empty, ended up with eight demons back in the house far worse than the one expelled! (verses 43-45).

Being conformed to the world involves far more than overt sins. Jesus is always searching our hearts to see what our attitudes and values really are. James (the brother of Jesus) wrote, "You adulterous people, don't you know that friendship with the world means enmity against God? Therefore, anyone who chooses to be a friend of the world becomes an enemy of God. Or do you think Scripture says without reason that he jealously longs for the spirit he has caused to dwell in us?" (James 4:4-5). A literal translation of the last sentence would be "anyone who wishes to be a friend of the world..." In other words, a person could secretly desire to hold on to the world's values and be just as guilty as if he had overtly pursued them. We will find ourselves destroyed if we outwardly conform to God's commands while inwardly conforming to Satan's offerings. The heart will ultimately come out and win out. We must deal with sin in our hearts if we are to reject the world. Confess it and crucify it.

After refusing to be conformed, we must volunteer to be transformed. The original word is the root from which we get our English word "metamorphosis." The change involved in a metamorphosis is profound. It is the difference between a caterpillar and a butterfly! God does not want people who are a little different in a few areas—he wants entirely new creations (2 Corinthians 5:17). "And we all, who with unveiled faces contemplate the Lord's glory, are being transformed into his image with ever-increasing glory, which comes from the Lord, who is the Spirit" (2 Corinthians 3:18).

This transformation has Christ as its model, for we are to imitate him in both character and behavior. Thus, there must be a *great* change, as a Jamaican song puts it. The change is also to be a continual one, for we never arrive at absolute Christlikeness. However, even though the changes are continual, we should avoid the conclusion that change in any one area must be gradual. Too many of us settle for changing slowly, when in fact, a radical repentance would result in rapid changes. If you end up maturing from a sinful or immature behavior gradually, don't let that be your default heart approach. Our heart's desire must be to change radically, quickly, and continually.

Praise God that he provides power behind our transforming! He forgives the sin; he provides the Spirit; and yet we must cooperate with the process by keeping our minds renewed, always keeping them set on him (Colossians 3:1-2). Paul's word to the Philippians applies to us today. He says, "Therefore, my dear friends, as you have always obeyed—not only in my presence, but now much more in my absence—continue to work out your salvation with fear and trembling, for it is God who works in you to will and to act in order to fulfill his good purpose" (Philippians 2:12-13). What we cannot do, he absolutely will do, if we allow him to have free reign in our lives.

The Results

The results of our sacrifice are totally satisfying—we can test and approve God's will and see that it is good, pleasing, and perfect. It is not simply good; nor just better than most paths of life; it is the best available life. But no one can prove it intellectually—it must be tested through obedience and submission. A similar progression is seen in John 8:31-32, where belief leads to holding to the truth, which in turn leads to knowing the truth, which finally results in freedom. No person ever knows truth who does not first *know* Jesus on an experiential level.

Sacrifice is a scary word. Surrender, even to God, is an unnatural decision from a human perspective. And yet death (to self) results in life which is life indeed. We become willing to yield our lives, our health, our family, our finances, our future, and our plans totally to him. We are willing to accept what we need rather than what we want. In essence, we allow God to *be* God in our lives as we make an emotional break with being in control. Sacrifice is an issue of trust, and trust is what faith is all about, and "without faith it is impossible to please him" (Hebrews 11:6). Sacrifice is not simply a lofty idea; it is the standard of following Jesus. Are you doing it? Will you be a living sacrifice?

QUESTIONS FOR THOUGHT

1. In what ways are you conformed to the world's values and actions? Be honest with yourself and pray about it as you contemplate your answers.

2. Some areas in which we need to transform fall into the realm of repentance and some fall into the realm of gradual change (even after repentance). In thinking of the areas of your life needing transformation: is something in your "gradual growth" category capable of being in the "repentance" and immediate change category?

3. How does the concept of surrender, letting go and letting God be in control, affect our ability to be a living sacrifice? Why does surrender work and why is it a challenge for you?

ACTION ITEMS

List three areas in your spiritual life that you feel good about right now, and three areas that most need improvement (transformation). Make a plan to take one step in each of these three latter areas this week and write down how you think you made progress. Also, give thanks to God for the three areas that you feel strong in and let that be a motivation to help you grow in the other three areas. Gratitude keeps Satan away from discouraging you.

CHAPTER TWELVE

Is Your Christian Life a Burden or a Blessing?

—Gordon Ferguson

The gospel of Christ is good news! In fact, it is great news! And, of course, good news is always worth sharing. But some may view the good news as bad news (or at least as mediocre news) and they will not be anxious to share it. Since many who wear the name of Christ do little or no sharing, something simply must be wrong with their view of the good news. Maybe their faith is a burden to them rather than a blessing.

What are the characteristics of someone whose faith is a burden? One, they likely have a negative view of obedience, perhaps secretly chafing at the idea of anyone (even God) telling them what to do. We live in a society which is bent on doing its own thing. "If it feels good, do it!" Therefore, words like "commandments" and "must" go against the grain of their spirits. They begin to pick and choose what they want to do, rather than really practicing the concept of "Thy will be done."

Two, behind this negative view of obedience lies a negative view of God. They think he is trying to stifle them and ruin their fun. So, they grimly hold on to their sour religion, hoping against hope that at least heaven will be some fun. The person with this frame of reference usually views heaven as better than hell, but not as good as life on earth. Thus, God is seen as robbing them of what they would secretly like to do. Since God is watching, however, they must behave, lest he slap them into hell. The "burdened" Christian sees God as primarily a Judge rather than as their Father. No wonder they don't share the good news: they have nothing good to share!

What causes someone to develop such a non-biblical, harmful way of thinking? Almost always, the concept can be traced back to the way they first viewed "church." Many youths are forced to be a part of something they don't understand. On Sundays, they are roused out of a sound sleep, ordered to eat and get dressed, then it's "off to church we go." Often, the child has experienced very little (or no) spirituality in the home during the week. They have noticed the Sunday morning atmosphere in the home is tense, and folks are irritable with one another, as if they resented the "duties" of the day. They have also overheard the negativism about the church leaders and others in the flock. And they have surely noticed the bulk of what they have been taught about the faith has majored in "don'ts" rather than "dos."

Of course, not all parents program their children to resent God and church in this manner, but too many do. We can force our children for only so long. If they don't understand the "whys" of what we are doing, they will ultimately reject the faith altogether, or inherit the negative "fire insurance religion" of their parents. Our children are amazingly perceptive about us. They know where our real values are, and they will probably adopt them when they are mature. If we love God with all our hearts, they likely will also, provided the love is obvious in our lives and in our words. We must communicate to them what life in Christ is all about, and not simply drag them to church.

Others come into the church from outside of Christian families, and they may also develop a burdened view of Christianity. Since the "seed reproduces after its own kind," they will become like others already in the body of Christ. If they see negative people, they will usually imitate them. If they see excited Christians, they will likely retain their zeal. In any event, our early concepts of what church is all about will normally stay with us for a long time. It takes real effort and determination to change erroneous concepts, because they are implanted more at the emotional level than at the intellectual level. We can know right yet feel wrong, especially where early concepts are concerned. However, change is possible. Praise God for that! We can learn to enjoy our walk with God!

Faith That is a Blessing

Now, what are the characteristics of one whose faith is a blessing? One, they are often a newer convert from outside of a Christian family. Thankfully, some raised in church families have this attitude also, but my experience has convinced me that a significant number of those "raised in the church" don't deeply feel this way. This is why newer converts are often more evangelistic than those from Christian homes. They have experienced the blessings of the good news and are anxious to share it.

Two, the person with a "blessed faith" loves God's commandments. In our day, the newer convert probably came out of an obviously sinful lifestyle. They know that Satan's enticements destroy rather than bless. They therefore see grace in its proper perspective. Rather than being resistant deep inside towards God's commands, they are grateful for the guidance of a loving Father who is trying to steer them away from pain. God has filled the void in their soul, and they are excited enough to want to share the good news with others. Lest this chapter seem too negative towards us "lifers" (as one brother called those of us raised in the church setting), let me say that there would not be any new converts unless others in the body of Christ taught them.

There are many excited Christians who have been in the Lord for many years. Praise God for you! You have fought Satan's attacks successfully, becoming stronger as a result. You have refused to lose your first love (Revelation 2:4) and to become lukewarm (Revelation 3:16). When many new converts have started cooling off, you have encouraged them by life and by word. Your religion is a blessing and not a burden.

However, no one will argue the fact that far too many Christians have a negative, burdened view of their faith. Being honest about the reality of the problem will allow us to do something to solve it. Playing "ostrich" with our heads in the sand is not God's way. We must be honest with ourselves and others if change is to come. Several suggestions are in order for helping us overcome a burdened view of Christianity.

Changing Your Perspective

First, we must develop a healthy view of God and His grace. He is not waiting for us to mess up; he is waiting for us to start developing a personal love relationship with him. Listening to sermons on grace, mercy, and love will help us a good deal. Reading positive books about Christ are of great benefit. Above all, pray to God by talking aloud with him as you would talk to any person whom you loved. Be open and honest. Pour out your heart. Don't say trite religious-sounding memorized phrases. Just talk to God and tell him how you really feel deep down inside. That's real prayer. Nothing else will suffice.

Second, begin thinking of the Bible as a *Book of Life* rather than a *Book of Religion.* It is practical and helpful in every area of life, from business to sexuality. God made us and speaks to our needs, whether great or small. He is trying to bless us, not stifle us. Learn to hunger and thirst after his words. Read for application to your life, not just for facts. You will begin to find things that are so helpful that you will want to share them with others!

Third, learn to overcome wrong things by doing right things. We cannot survive on a religion of "don'ts." Overcome evil with good. God shows this approach clearly in Ephesians 4:25-32. Replace falsehood with speaking truth. Replace stealing with working to give to others in need. Replace unwholesome words with saying only what will build others up. Replace anger and slander with kindness and forgiveness. Practice a positive Christian walk rather than simply avoiding negatives.

Fourth, learn to verbalize more to your family about God and his positive blessings. As Moses said in Deuteronomy 6:5-7, we must first love God with all our being, do what he says, and then talk about it as a normal part of everyday life. Sharing God with others was never intended to be a fearful burden, but an exciting blessing. Sharing good news is natural if we really view it as good news. Satan is pleased if we view our Christian walk as a grim duty. God is pleased if we view it as a blessing. Let's make God happy. He deserves it!

QUESTIONS FOR THOUGHT

1. Do you wake up most days feeling burdened? How often do you wake up feeling on fire for God and energized to share about your relationship with him?

2. How do we extenuate the positive aspects of our faith?

3. What are some ways to overcome negative aspects of our walk with God?

ACTION ITEMS

Set up a lunch with the most positive Christian you know. Ask them how they stay positive. Then put that into practice.

CHAPTER THIRTEEN

Forever Growing

—Theresa Ferguson

"Therefore we do not lose heart. Though outwardly we are wasting away, yet inwardly we are being renewed day by day. For our light and momentary troubles are achieving for us an eternal glory that far outweighs them all. So we fix our eyes not on what is seen, but on what is unseen, since what is seen is temporary, but what is unseen is eternal." (2 Corinthians 4:16-18)

Personal growth is our key to living an abundant Christian life. As we age, our bodies may be "wasting away, yet inwardly we are being renewed day by day" (2 Corinthians 4:16). Even as an 81-year-old woman, I am constantly being inspired and challenged with the realization that God expects and enables me to grow daily. As women in the kingdom of God, to be forever growing is to be forever excited! In this chapter, I want to mention four keys to that continual growth.

Leave Childishness and Learn Childlikeness

1 Corinthians 13:11 is our admonition to mature and accept responsibility for our own growth. We must decide to put to death our childish talk, thinking and reasoning. We need to take seriously such sins as self-pity, unwholesome talk, criticalness, whining, complaining, and blame-shifting. Too many women, even Christians, behave like spoiled children in both attitudes and actions. How does your childishness show itself?

Matthew 18:2-4 states that we must become humble like a little child to enter and be great in God's kingdom. We must be willing to learn from anyone regardless of their role or our own role in the kingdom. Also, we need to trust in God completely to enable us to grow and, most importantly, we need to trust the people he has put in our life to help us change. Ultimately, if we do not trust these people, we do not trust God. To the extent that I trust my Bible and those helping me in my faith, I am trusting God.

Open Your Life to God's Discipling

Romans 5: 1-8 has helped me to see that God disciples us through our circumstances and struggles. We develop character, perseverance and hope in our lives through struggles. I have learned to thank God for the struggles because my heart is exposed during these times of testing. How do you view struggles? Do you see God's hand in them to mature you, or do you view them as burdens to be avoided at all costs? Depending on which view you accept, you will be helped or hurt by the struggles.

2 Peter 1:3-8 assures us that God's divine power and promises enable us to grow in our faith, goodness, knowledge, self-control, perseverance, godliness, brotherly kindness and love. If we make every effort to grow in these qualities, the result will be a productive, effective knowledge of Jesus Christ. But we must be willing to pay the price of perseverance, for these qualities are not developed easily nor quickly.

Be Victorious Over Character Weaknesses

We must be aware of our character weaknesses and decide to throw them off (Hebrews 12:1). This awareness is developed by our own decision to be honest about our attitudes and motives, along with our openness to have others evaluate our behavior. Once these weaknesses are identified, we start getting rid of them by replacing them with corresponding strengths. Colossians 3:14 describes this process as "putting off" sins and "putting on" righteousness.

We also gain victory over these weaknesses by imitating successes. Many biblical characters turned weakness into strength. Hebrews 11 is a Hall of Fame of individuals who struggled but with power from God were overcomers. So many in fact that the Hebrew writer says:

Hebrews 11:32-39

[32] And what more shall I say? I do not have time to tell about Gideon, Barak, Samson and Jephthah, about David and Samuel and the prophets, [33] who through faith conquered kingdoms, administered justice, and gained what was promised; who shut the mouths of lions, [34] quenched the fury of the flames, and escaped the edge of the sword; whose weakness was turned to strength; and who became powerful in battle and routed foreign armies. [35] Women received back their dead, raised to life again. There were others who were tortured, refusing to be released so that they might gain an even better resurrection. [36] Some faced jeers and flogging, and even chains and imprisonment. [37] They were put to death by stoning; they were sawed in two; they were killed by the sword. They went about in sheepskins and goatskins, destitute, persecuted and mistreated— [38] the world was not worthy of them. They wandered in deserts and mountains, living in caves and in holes in the ground. [39] These were all commended for their faith.

What a Hall of Fame of effectual faith. But even above and beyond these amazing folks, we have the perfect example of the spiritual strength in Jesus. A continual study of his life is an absolute must to inspire our faith. Keep repenting, keep studying and keep imitating to see your character genuinely change.

Be Eager to Help Others Grow

Our key motivation in helping others grow is for their own good. But when we help them, God rewards us with personal growth as well. When we struggle with them to help them overcome their sins, we deepen our own convictions about sin and righteousness. This is something that Paul reminded the Colossians about: "He is the one we proclaim, admonishing and teaching everyone with all wisdom, so that we may present everyone fully mature in Christ. To this end I strenuously contend with all the energy Christ so powerfully works in me" (Colossians 1:28-29). When we strive to instill vision in others, we gain hope for our lives. When we use biblical principles to encourage them, we find ourselves also encouraged, for these principles apply to everyone equally. While it is "more blessed to give than to receive," it is impossible to give without receiving in return (Luke 6:38).

Therefore, when we leave childishness, open our lives to God, claim victory over weaknesses, and are eager to help others grow, we will forever grow in love. May God help us to grow daily, that we may continually love others into his kingdom!

QUESTIONS FOR THOUGHT

1. Are you self-motivated in your desire to grow or do you continually have to be prodded by others?

2. Do you willingly confess your inner thoughts and feelings to your friends? Do you encourage transparency by setting the example in openness?

3. Are you eager to help others grow? Do they know that you believe in them?

ACTION ITEMS

Gather a group of your Christian friends. Have each person share how they have grown the most during the last twelve months. Then everyone can share what area they most need to grow in now and make a plan to make it happen.

CHAPTER FOURTEEN

Reviving the Spirit of Joy

—Theresa Ferguson

"Will you not revive us again, that your people may rejoice in you? Show us your unfailing love, Lord, and grant us your salvation." (Psalm 85:6-7)

God intends for us to live a joy-filled life! He gives us true joy at the time of our conversion, and he will revive our joy daily. When we are joyful, others will be drawn to the Christian life. The point of this chapter is to help us understand what Christian joy is all about, with an emphasis on how to revive a joy that has lost its luster.

What is Joy?

The popular concept of joy centers around a sense of excitement and happiness which is based on outward circumstances. In other words, we are joyful because everything is going our way. Conversely, we are expected to be saddened when a disappointment comes down our path. Biblical joy, however, has little dependence on outward events. Amid persecution and rejection, Jesus was characterized by joy (John 15:11). In the bleak discomfort of living as a prisoner, Paul wrote that we should rejoice (Philippians 4:4). In fact, he commanded that we should be joyful always (1 Thessalonians 5:16)! Clearly, Christian joy and worldly joy are miles apart.

Our joy is not based on our performance but on God's acceptance—our names are written in heaven (Luke 10:20). From the moment of our salvation onward, everything God does in our lives is designed to mold us into his image. With this assurance in our hearts, we can consider it pure joy even as we face hardships

(James 1:2)! Joy, then, is our enthusiastic and grateful response to the promises of God to always work for our best spiritual interests. Whether it feels like it or not, we can be assured that this is God's purpose and plan for us.

Have I Lost My Joy?

If you have lost your joy, the loss was likely a gradual one. Satan knows how to gradually cool down anything that is good. One day we take a good look in the mirror and exclaim, "Where did my joy go?" The loss of joy manifests itself in several ways. One, we talk less about Jesus and what he has done in our lives. If the mouth speaks out of the overflow of the heart (Luke 6:45), then a lack of joy directly impacts our sharing. What does your level of evangelism say about your level of joy?

Also, we lose our depth of gratitude to God for our salvation. Certainly, thankfulness is one of the greatest Christian virtues, but when our joy fades, our sense of appreciation follows closely behind. Just how thankful have you been in your life recently? How have you demonstrated it? Additionally, our general countenance shows how joyful we are. Faces can be read, and they usually tell the story of what is going on in the inner person. When we have no joy, we are usually downcast. As Solomon said, "A happy heart makes the face cheerful, but heartache crushes the spirit" (Proverbs 15:13). How is your face looking these days? Ask someone close to you to help you evaluate your level of joy. We sometimes fool ourselves more easily than we fool those around us.

How Did I Lose My Joy?

We lose our joy by losing our focus. Our eyes must be set on Christ and things above. Paul said: "Since, then, you have been raised with Christ, set your hearts on things above, where Christ is, seated at the right hand of God. Set your minds on things above, not on earthly things" (Colossians 3:1-2). We sometimes forget that our mission is to make and mature disciples (Matthew 28:19-20). When we begin to focus on earthly physical things instead of heavenly and spiritual ones, we will surely lose our joy. A lack of focus will lead to a loss of faith in God to use us. We begin to listen to the lies of Satan instead of the promises of God. We then begin concealing sin in our hearts from God and our fellow disciples and we even deceive ourselves. Satan is the great deceiver, and he knows how to steal our joy without us knowing that it is gone. Where is your focus right now? If it is not on things above, you have lost your joy!

How Do I Revive My Joy?

Thankfully, we can revive our joy. The book of Psalms provides key principles to help us restore joy in our lives. Since our joy comes from God: One, we can cry out asking him to take over control of our lives; to totally surrender and trust in him to revive our joy. The Psalmist says, "Bring joy to your servant, Lord, for I put my trust in you" (Psalm 86:4). The Apostle Peter also reminds us, "Cast all your anxiety on him because he cares for you" (1 Peter 5:7).

Two, we confess, repent, and renounce our sins so that forgiveness and refreshment can produce joy. King David experienced this as he confessed and renounced his sin. "Against you, you only, have I sinned and done what is evil in your sight... Cleanse me with hyssop, and I will be clean; wash me, and I will be whiter than snow. Let me hear joy and gladness; let the bones you have crushed rejoice...Create in me a pure heart, O God, and renew a steadfast spirit within me...Restore to me the joy of your salvation and grant me a willing spirit, to sustain me. Then I will teach transgressors your ways, so that sinners will turn back to you" (Psalm 51:1-13, excerpts).

Three, we let "love and faithfulness" fill our lives, and we let "righteousness and peace kiss each other" in our lives (Psalm 85:10). Four, we count our blessings and praise God for the miracles of a changed life (Psalm 86:8-10). Five, we share our joy daily with others in our circle of friends and in every situation we enter. Helping someone know our source of joy is one of the most exciting parts of reviving our joy (Psalm 51:13).

God will revive us again. Decide daily to set your mind and

heart to be like Jesus. When we do, we will be joy-filled people! Joy has a way of ushering in that peace of God that transcends all understanding (Philippians 4:7). Whatever the price of revival, the rewards will far exceed it!

QUESTIONS FOR THOUGHT

1. How would friends describe your demeanor? Is joyful one of the first adjectives that they mention?

2. What impact does bad news usually have on your psyche and how do you react?

3. Since sin steals our joy—how quick are you to confess your sins? Do you typically conceal or confess sin?

ACTION ITEMS

In your quiet time, take an inventory of your joy level. Is it bursting out? Does it brighten a room? Does it lead others to God? Does it reflect a closeness to Jesus? After taking an assessment, share that information with your friends in Christ.

CHAPTER FIFTEEN

Faith in Closed Doors

—Gordon Ferguson

The New Testament mentions "open" doors a number of times. For example, 2 Corinthians 2:12 says of Paul, "Now when I went to Troas to preach the gospel of Christ and found that the Lord had opened a door for me…" Acts 14:27 says this, "On arriving there, they gathered the church together and reported all that God had done through them and how he had opened the door of faith to the Gentiles." We love open doors; they indeed build our faith. However, how we view closed doors is our real challenge. It is easy to have faith in open doors, but having faith in closed doors is a faith that has to be developed. Paul developed a remarkable faith in closed doors, which demonstrates far greater faith in God than do open doors. By examining examples from his life, we can learn to imitate his faith in closed doors, the type of faith that we are going to need many, many times in our walk with God.

Closed Doors to His Early Preaching

First, Paul had to deal with closed doors to his early preaching. His conversion and early activities in the church are described first in Acts 9 in quite some detail and recounted by Paul in both Acts 22 and 26 when making a defense before Jewish and then Roman officials. Zealot that he was, Paul began preaching immediately in Damascus right after his conversion, which soon led to a conspiracy by the Jews to kill him, resulting in him being lowered in a basket through an opening in the wall in the middle of the night (Acts 9:20-25). We might have expected that the conversion of the biggest enemy of Christianity might have served to open the ears and hearts of those Jews, but it was quite the opposite.

According to the next verses in Acts 9:26-30, Paul went to Jerusalem and found doors to his message closed as well, starting with the apostles who were afraid that he was carrying out a "Trojan Horse" scheme. Thankfully, the "Son of Encouragement" (Barnabas) was on the scene and persuaded the apostles that Paul's conversion was the real deal. As Paul began preaching in this very center of Judaism, and debated with the Hellenistic Jews, they too tried to kill him. This led to the disciples taking him down to Caesarea and sending him off to Tarsus. Throughout Paul's entire life as a Christian, he encountered far more closed doors to his message than open ones, and many of the former were violently closed. So what was Paul's response to this? He never stopped preaching and teaching, for he was the master imitator of Jesus! He refused to allow rejection to quench his faith in closed doors, believing that open doors were soon to come (and they did).

Closed Doors to Mission Work

Acts 16:6-10 is a remarkable passage about Paul's faith when his plans for mission work were seemingly blocked.

Acts 16:6-10

⁶ Paul and his companions traveled throughout the region of Phrygia and Galatia, having been kept by the Holy Spirit from preaching the word in the province of Asia. ⁷ When they came to the border of Mysia, they tried to enter Bithynia, but the Spirit of Jesus would not allow them to. ⁸ So they passed by Mysia and went down to Troas. ⁹ During the night Paul had a vision of a man of Macedonia standing and begging him, "Come over to Macedonia and help us." ¹⁰ After Paul had seen the vision, we got ready at once to leave for Macedonia, concluding that God had called us to preach the gospel to them.

Some might have become discouraged after two sets of plans were blocked, but not Paul. His plan for what we call his second missionary journey was to go to Asia, which by human logic was an excellent plan. Ephesus was in Asia and one of the major cities of the Roman Empire, an ideal place to set up a beachhead for spreading the gospel all over Asia. In fact, this is exactly what

Paul did on his third mission trip (Acts 19). But God had other plans for his second journey, and Paul had to trust that God would indeed make his plans clear. Notice in Acts 16:10 how quickly Paul recognized that plan when it presented itself in a vision: "we got ready at once" to leave for Macedonia. What we begin seeing is the principle that when God closes one door, he opens another one—and usually a much better one! The Lord knows that all of us need to develop that kind of faith in closed doors rather than allowing disappointment to discourage us when "our" plan fails. We must trust that God has a better one waiting in the wings and will in his time reveal it to us.

Closed Doors to Paul's Freedom

Acts 16:16-34 describe Paul's preaching in Philippi which led to his arrest and beating with rods, leaving him bleeding in the inner cell of a jail with his feet fastened in stocks (along with Silas). This may have been Paul's first experience in a jail cell, but it was far from his last. His arrest in Jerusalem likely led to him being detained for the night in the prison at the Fortress of Antonia (Acts 22). From there, he was taken to Caesarea in the middle of the night to escape the Jews who had taken a vow to fast until they had killed him (Acts 23). He ended up remaining in prison there for over two years. Next, he was taken to Rome and was imprisoned there two different times. Whether he spent time in other jails we are not told, but doors to freedom were often closed for Paul and remained closed for a number of years. He said in 2 Corinthians 11:23, in comparing himself to his false apostle enemies, that he "been in prison more frequently" than they.

Did closed prison doors threaten Paul's faith? Not at all. He did some of his best work in prison. For starters, we have four "Prison Epistles" as a result (Ephesians, Philippians, Colossians, and Philemon). The miraculous conversion of the Philippian jailor and his family in Acts 16 provides us with one of the most important conversion accounts in the Book of Acts. While jailed in Caesarea, he had the opportunity to speak on more than one occasion to Roman officials of high rank, in fulfillment of Jesus' words in Mark 12:9 and Acts 9:15. In jail, he was constantly guarded by Roman soldiers. And how did that work out for Paul and for them?

Read it.

Philippians 1:12-13
¹² Now I want you to know, brothers and sisters, that what has happened to me has actually served to advance the gospel. ¹³ As a result, it has become clear throughout the whole palace guard and to everyone else that I am in chains for Christ.

Philippians 4:22
²² All God's people here send you greetings, especially those who belong to Caesar's household.

When in jail, Paul literally had a captive audience, resulting in some of even Caesar's household being converted. In the final two verses of Acts, we read these thrilling words describing his first imprisonment in Rome.

Acts 28:30-31
³⁰ For two whole years Paul stayed there in his own rented house and welcomed all who came to see him. ³¹ He proclaimed the kingdom of God and taught about the Lord Jesus Christ—with all boldness and without hindrance!

What About Us?
Why are closed doors such a challenge? We too easily think, "It's closed, so that must be what God wants." Yet, Matthew 7:7-8 contains a very clear promise. "Ask and it will be given to you; seek and you will find; knock and the door will be opened to you. For everyone who asks receives; the one who seeks finds; and to the one who knocks, the door will be opened." We Americans have very short attention spans and patience. We are short-term in our expectations and give up very quickly if God doesn't answer our prayers the way we expect.

Obviously, we need to develop a big picture view of what God is doing in our lives. We need a healthy dose of trust in the promises in Romans 8:28-29. What are your closed doors that you need to face with faith right now? Maybe it's character change in yourself. Maybe it's changes in others—radical changes like being saved or the same type of character changes in fellow disciples that you need to make yourself. Maybe it's about your health challenges; or your financial challenges. Maybe it's your evangelism efforts or effectiveness. Maybe it's your marriage or other relationships in your physical family, or perhaps relationships in your spiritual family.

The point is that we all have them, one sort of closed door or another, and we desperately need to develop the faith in closed doors that Paul had in such an amazing way—that God will open the door in unexpected ways or open a better door. God wants to open doors for you, especially the kind that seem that they cannot be opened. Another way of looking at that truth is to realize that God wants your faith muscles to develop you into a superman or superwoman of faith, and to use you in ways far beyond your ability to comprehend now. Let's make the decision to fully cooperate with his desire to do just that!

QUESTIONS FOR THOUGHT

1. What about Paul's faith in closed doors thrilled you most? Why?

2. When God doesn't answer your prayer requests quickly or in the way you asked them, how does this affect your faith?

3. Can you think of times when you were initially disappointed that your prayer requests weren't answered and yet later you thanked God that they weren't?

ACTION ITEMS

Read and study Romans 8:28-29 and then make a list of times when closed doors to your prayers resulted in significant spiritual growth. Remember that spiritual growth and challenges are most often inseparably joined!

CHAPTER SIXTEEN

Keeping the Tongue from Evil— Unwholesome Talk, Part 1

—Gordon Ferguson

> "The tongue also is a fire, a world of evil among the parts of
> the body. It corrupts the whole person, sets the whole course
> of his life on fire, and is itself set on fire by hell." (James 3:6)

It would be difficult to find a more shocking verse about the use of the tongue. Talking is something we all do daily, in abundance. No wonder the writer of Proverbs said, "When words are many, sin is not absent" (Proverbs 10:19). Of course, the reverse effect of the tongue is also duly noted in Proverbs 16:24: "Pleasant words are a honeycomb, sweet to the soul and healing to the bones." Words used wrongly are a curse, while words used correctly are a blessing, as Proverbs 18:21 states: "The tongue has the power of life and death, and those who love it will eat its fruit."

It is imperative that we understand the difference between the two types of talk, for Satan in his deceitfulness can confuse us and deceive us into using the wrong kind of talk—sometimes without us even realizing what we are doing. The purpose of the next two chapters is to enable us to recognize in ourselves and in others what unwholesome talk is so that we can avoid it like the plague.

Since life is all about relationships, and relationships are, in large part, based on communication, we are not surprised by the multitude of biblical passages that focus on correct and incorrect communication. Consider this excellent passage that describes both sides of the conversation coin:

Ephesians 4:29-32

[29] Do not let any unwholesome talk come out of your mouths, but only what is helpful for building others up according to their needs, that it may benefit those who listen. [30] And do not grieve the Holy Spirit of God, with whom you were sealed for the day of redemption. [31] Get rid of all bitterness, rage and anger, brawling and slander, along with every form of malice. [32] Be kind and compassionate to one another, forgiving each other, just as in Christ God forgave you.

We Will Hurt One Another With Our Words

Sadly, this is an unavoidable truth regarding all long-term relationships. Just ask any husband and wife, or any parent and child. Often, we hurt one another in completely unintentional ways. Perhaps that's why James made this observation in James 3:2: "Anyone who is never at fault in what they say is perfect." While sometimes our hurtful communication is unintentional, there are other times we know our words are damaging. Deep down inside our hearts we know we are talking in ways we wouldn't want made public. Our consciences speak to us clearly in such cases.

This type of speech is called gossip and slander in the Bible. Here are a few key verses about this type of sinful speech:

Proverbs 18:8: The words of a gossip are like choice morsels; they go down to a man's inmost parts.

Proverbs 12:18-19: Reckless words pierce like a sword, but the tongue of the wise brings healing. Truthful lips endure forever, but a lying tongue lasts only a moment.

Proverbs 15:4: The tongue that brings healing is a tree of life, but a deceitful tongue crushes the spirit.

Proverbs 16:28: A perverse man stirs up dissension, and a gossip separates close friends.

Proverbs 26:22-25: The words of a gossip are like choice morsels; they go down to a man's inmost parts. Like a coating of glaze over earthenware are fervent lips with an evil heart. A malicious man disguises himself with his lips, but in his heart he harbors deceit. Though his speech is charming, do not believe him, for seven abominations fill his heart.

Proverbs 26:28: A lying tongue hates those it hurts, and a flattering mouth works ruin.

Proverbs 20:19: A gossip betrays a confidence; so avoid anyone who talks too much.

Psalm 55:21: His speech is smooth as butter, yet war is in his heart; his words are more soothing than oil, yet they are drawn swords.

Jeremiah 9:8: Their tongue is a deadly arrow; it speaks deceitfully. With their mouths they all speak cordially to their neighbors, but in their hearts they set traps for them.

Especially serious to God is hurtful talk about his leaders. Beginning in Eden when the serpent tempted Eve to lose trust in her Leader and Creator, Satan has continued to tempt us into distrusting and even slandering our leaders. Contrary to popular practice, God doesn't want us to speak negatively even about our political leaders. Paul makes this principle clear in Titus 3:1-2 in these terms: "Remind the people to be subject to rulers and authorities, to be obedient, to be ready to do whatever is good, to slander no one, to be peaceable and considerate, and to show true humility toward all men." Now, if God doesn't want us speaking negatively about political leaders, we should not be surprised when he forbids speaking against leaders in his spiritual family. Listen to 1 Timothy 5:19, as Paul writes the following: "Do not receive an accusation against an elder except on the basis of two or three witnesses."

We Rationalize When We Speak or Listen Sinfully

As stated already, we usually are quite aware of it when we are guilty of gossip and slander. This awareness is evidenced by how we introduce such speech. Here are some common examples:

"You know, I just have some things on my heart that I need to share with someone, and you are one of my best friends."

"I need a safe place and a safe person to share some concerns that are really troubling me. Can you be that safe person and keep what I tell you confidential?"

"I don't feel like I have anyone who really understands what I am feeling, and I'm so happy to have you as a confidential friend who can listen and keep a confidence."

Hearing those types of introductions, we normally feel concern for the speaker and want to help, and we feel flattered that we are that chosen friend to whom this person can unburden their hearts. But the problem with what then takes place is that the talker is sinning and we as a listener are also sinning! And then, of course, we must find ways to justify both the sin of the speaker and our own sin of listening. Our justifications go something like this: "Well, he just got emotional and needed to work through it." "She just said that terrible thing because she was angry."

So, being emotional makes it not sinful? Try this excuse on for size: "I just got emotional and shot that guy, but it was because I was overly emotional, so it wasn't wrong!" And the claim that someone says something just because they are angry is absolute nonsense. Whatever we say, whether calm or angry, is said because it is in our heart. Jesus made that abundantly clear in Luke 6:45: "Out of the overflow of his heart his mouth speaks." We don't say things just because we are emotional—we say them because they are in our hearts, and our emotions remove our inhibitions! We may think that listening to someone spew out their negativity is helpful to them and not affecting us, but sins of speech affect all participants in more ways than we imagine.

QUESTIONS FOR THOUGHT

1. Are you prone to gossip? Do you invite people to share confidences about others?

2. The scripture says that the tongue of the wise brings healing. What are some of the ways your words can bring healing in your life setting?

3. How do we justify repeating or listening to gossip?

ACTION ITEMS

Review the last three months. Was there a time when you listened to or repeated gossip about someone you know. If yes, then go to that person and ask for their forgiveness. (This is true repentance.)

CHAPTER SEVENTEEN

Keeping the Tongue from Evil—
Unwholesome Talk, Part 2

—Gordon Ferguson

"The tongue also is a fire, a world of evil among the parts of
the body. It corrupts the whole person, sets the whole course
of his life on fire, and is itself set on fire by hell." (James 3:6)

What is God's Solution to Unwholesome Talk?

First, avoid it yourself. Before sharing sensitive details about
another person's life without their knowledge, ask yourself the
following questions:

Why are you considering sharing these things?
Will your sharing benefit the one you are sharing about?
Will it benefit the one with whom you are sharing?
Will it bring glory to God and his kingdom?
Would you want the same thing shared about your own life?
Does the Golden Rule (Luke 6:31) fit the situation?

It would also be wise to remember what Paul said in Ephesians 4:29: "Do not let any unwholesome talk come out of your
mouths, but only what is helpful for building others up according
to their needs, that it may benefit those who listen."

Second, refuse to participate in the sinful speech of another
by being a willing listener. Here are some responses you can have
that are righteous when such talk begins:

"Wait a minute–I am not comfortable with hearing negative talk about someone who is not here and able to give

their side of the story." (You do remember what Proverbs 18:17 says, right? "The first to present his case seems right, till another comes forward and questions him.")

"Have you shared this with the person themselves?" (On this one, you must be very thorough. They may say, "Yes I have told them this" when they really haven't. Or they have hinted about it but not really said directly what they are now saying to you.)

Then say, "Well, if you have told them this, I will want to talk with them about it later to make sure I hear their side of the story, based on Proverbs 18:17."

Truthfully, even if they have told the other person, why are they telling you? Saying, "Well, I'm not saying anything to you that I haven't already said to them," doesn't make it right to repeat something negative to you. It is still a violation of the Golden Rule! If they say, "No, I haven't told them because they wouldn't handle it well, so I need to share it with you as a confidential person to just unburden my heart," then you have to intervene and stop the gossip. You should then say, "You do have to go and share this with the other person, based on the commands of Jesus. If you need me to go with you, I will go, but you need to do what Jesus says." I then ask, "Will you go? When will you go? And if they say they will go, I follow up to make sure that they did. If they say that they won't go, I say, "If you haven't obeyed Jesus and gone to them within a week, I am going to go and share with them what you have said, to make sure you two get together and work this out."

Now why would I do all of this? You have to admit that it sounds rather drastic to some (most?) of you, and very different from the way you have often done it and seen it done—right? Bottom line, it is a matter of obeying the Lord Jesus Christ.

Listen To Jesus' Solution for All of Our Relationship Problems

Matthew 18:15-17

 [15] "If your brother or sister sins, go and point out their fault, just between the two of you. If they listen to you, you have won them over. [16] But if they will not listen, take one or two others along, so that 'every matter may be established by the testimony of two or three witnesses.' [17] If they still refuse to listen, tell it to the church; and if they refuse to listen even to the church, treat them as you would a pagan or a tax collector.

Matthew 5:23-24

[23] "Therefore, if you are offering your gift at the altar and there remember that your brother or sister has something against you, [24] leave your gift there in front of the altar. First go and be reconciled to them; then come and offer your gift.

Taking these two passages together, we might use an insurance term and say that they form Jesus' "double indemnity" guarantee. This "policy" renders continuing rifts in relationships between his followers impossible (and it would be impossible if we just obeyed him)! His solution may sound extremely challenging to us because we are, by nature, people pleasers and conflict avoiders; but it is the only option we have if we intend to live as disciples of Jesus Christ. I have committed myself to help resolve issues and relationships in the leadership of churches of which I have been a part. And I am just as intent on doing this with all of us in any church who need help, because we are the family of God. As God's children, we must strive for the complete unity for which Christ prayed (John 17:23) and ultimately died. Unity is destroyed by the wrong kind of speech but forged by the right kinds of speech. I also believe unity and healing can be experienced through the right kinds of resolution and reconciliation processes.

Therefore, watch your speech and how you live; and don't sin against one another. Train yourself to be a good listener and be sensitive when the speech of others begins heading in a sinful direction. Refuse to listen to it. Love the one talking to you enough to insist that they get resolved with those about whom they are tempted to talk negatively. We have to protect our souls and the souls of others with our speech and with the speech by others that we refuse to engage in. It is not easy, but it is the way of God, and we really have no options in the matter—we must obey him. The following passages provides us with the qualities necessary to build and maintain unity. Let's put it into practice!

Ephesians 4:1-6

¹ As a prisoner for the Lord, then, I urge you to live a life worthy of the calling you have received. ² Be completely humble and gentle; be patient, bearing with one another in love.

³ Make every effort to keep the unity of the Spirit through the bond of peace. ⁴ There is one body and one Spirit, just as you were called to one hope when you were called; ⁵ one Lord, one faith, one baptism; ⁶ one God and Father of all, who is over all and through all and in all.

QUESTIONS FOR THOUGHT

1. How can we share corrective ideas with others in such a way that it builds them up instead of tearing them down?

2. How does gossip destroy the unity of the church? Make a list.

3. When was the last time you went and talked to someone who had a problem with you, or you had a problem with them? How did it turn out?

ACTION ITEMS

Make a list of anyone who you think may have a problem with you. Set up a meeting with them this week and get it resolved!

CHAPTER EIGHTEEN

Encouraging One Another Daily

—Theresa Ferguson

"But encourage one another daily, as long as it is called Today, so that none of you may be hardened by sin's deceitfulness." (Hebrews 3:13)

If I asked the question, "Who needs to be encouraged?" the
unanimous answer would be "everyone" (especially *me*!). Yes, we
all need copious amounts of it, but it is also a command of God
for *every* disciple to be an encourager. We tend to look to leaders
and mature disciples for encouragement, without realizing that the
newest disciple has a similar responsibility. Encouragement is not
something we wait expectantly to receive—it is something we expect to give to others. And as with all spiritual qualities, it is more
blessed to give them than to receive. We *feel* encouraged when we
give encouragement! The English word *encourage* means "to put
courage in; to replace and instill courage; to build up or urge forward; to stir up, spur on, stimulate, refresh; to inspire with courage, spirit or hope."

When does God expect us to be encouragers? In a word: *daily.*
The hard part is to keep it on our hearts daily in a way that motivates us to practice it daily. Our selfish nature makes us much
more conscious of our own need to be encouraged than to think
about giving encouragement. The key to victory in this area is to
first get encouragement from our time with God, for only then do
we have something to share. Next, we seek to imitate God through
the earthly life of Jesus, learning to be disciples that daily spur
others on to victory.

Why did God give such a command in the first place? Hebrews 3:12-14 provides us with some great reasons. Encourage-

ment prevents disciples from developing a "sinful, unbelieving heart that turns away from the living God," and it ensures "that none of you may be hardened by sin's deceitfulness." We are thus enabled to "hold firmly till the end the confidence we had at first." Encouragement is our weapon against Satan as we use God's promises to help each other fend off the devil's schemes to weaken and destroy. We are instruments of God (Romans 6:13) to be the heart-lifters, faith-instillers, and spiritual-inspirers for his children. Our effectiveness is guaranteed by the Encourager (*Parakletos*) given to us at baptism, the Holy Spirit.

How can we all become excellent encouragers? Romans 12:8 tells us that encouragement is a special gift given to certain people by the Spirit. Thus, we need to seek out and imitate those who excel in this gift. Those who have it are readily recognizable.

1. Encouragers focus on God. They see life from the perspective of an all-powerful, all-loving God, not from the limitations of mortal men. As John put it in 1 John 4:4, "Greater is he who is in you than he who is in the world."

2. Encouragers are great listeners. They want to hear what is in your heart rather than dispense pat answers. They want to listen to your words and your feelings. All of us should simply strive to be like God, for he is the greatest listener of all (Psalm 10:17-18).

3. Encouragers are genuine and specific in their praise of others. Flattery may appear appealing, but it has no lasting effect. A real encourager explains why you can be victorious and helps you learn to think about your life with God's perspective.

4. Encouragers are aware of the needs of others to the point that they always initiate to meet those needs. I remember my hospitalizations through the years when the sight of a familiar face lifted my heart like nothing else could. I remember times when I felt overwhelmed by too many chores and too little time to do them. Then a knock came at the door. When I opened it, I was met by a smiling, unexpected angel with

rubber gloves and a bucket in her hands. Paul must have felt similar emotions when the brothers went to great lengths to encourage him as he traveled to Rome as a prisoner. Acts 28:15 reads: "The brothers and sisters there had heard that we were coming, and they traveled as far as the Forum of Appius and the Three Taverns to meet us. At the sight of these men Paul thanked God and was encouraged."

5. Encouragers are sacrificial. The example of Barnabas, whose name means "Son of Encouragement," demonstrates this point well. We first meet him in Acts 4:36-37 when he sold a field and gave the money to meet the needs of his brothers and sisters. Just imagine what gratitude those early disciples must have felt for Barnabas!

6. Encouragers have great vision for others. Again, Barnabas provides us with a powerful example. After Paul's conversion, he visited Jerusalem, only to discover that Jesus' apostles were afraid of him. However, it was Barnabas who persuaded them to accept Paul (Acts 9:26-27). Later, Barnabas brought him to help evangelize Antioch (Acts 11:25-26). No doubt his acceptance and encouragement of Paul had much to do with the amazingly effective apostle he became!

7. Encouragers are not sentimental or overly protective. Peter did not encourage Jesus when he tried to persuade Jesus not to go to the cross (Matthew 16:22-23), no matter how noble Peter's intentions may have seemed. True biblical encouragement points others in the direction of the cross, which by its nature is not easy. Paul and Barnabas offered sober counsel as they traveled, "strengthening the disciples and encouraging them to remain true to the faith. We must go through many hardships to enter the kingdom of God,' they said" (Acts 14:22).

8. Encouragers offer hope to others by sharing openly from their own lives. Nothing encourages others quite like being allowed into the hearts and lives of those offering help. Hearing about past defeats and victories of the presently strong

imparts tremendous hope to those who are presently weaker.

In conclusion, set your heart on becoming a great encourager of other people. On the Day of Judgment, many will rise up to call you blessed. When we have imitated those like Jesus, Paul and Barnabas, we will produce this heart-warming response in those whom we seek to encourage: "I am greatly encouraged; in all our troubles my joy knows no bounds" (2 Corinthians 7:4).

QUESTIONS FOR THOUGHT

1. Looking at the eight qualities of encouragers, what are your strongest points and your weakest points?

2. What have others done that encouraged you the most, and how well do you receive encouragement from others? If you are uncomfortable receiving it, remember that you are blessing the person offering it. They are finding joy in using their special gift, and it is more blessed to give then receive.

3. How can you tell when others need to be encouraged (write down your answers)?

ACTION ITEMS

Share your findings with someone who has a gift of encouragement and knows you well, then ask them their opinion about your answers. From there, make out a plan to encourage specific people daily.

CHAPTER NINETEEN

Hungry and Happy!

—Theresa Ferguson

"Blessed are those who hunger and thirst for righteousness, for they will be filled." (Matthew 5:6)

In looking at the high calling of the Beatitudes spoken by Jesus, some questions are in order. Do you really want true happiness? Are you willing to do whatever it takes to get true fulfillment? It is our response to Matthew 5:6 that will determine our joy level now and for as long as we live. From a worldly perspective, being hungry and happy at the same time does not seem correct. However, in the kingdom, we cannot be truly happy (blessed) without first being hungry—hungry for God! But what does this phrase mean in a practical sense?

In the preceding context, Jesus had been performing miracles and meeting many physical needs (Matthew 4:23-25). The people were happy and impressed with both his message and his miracles. They were hungry and thirsty to have their physical needs met, but like most of us, their spiritual interest may not have been their primary focus. He wanted them to know that they could have lasting fulfillment only if they were hungry and thirsty to be filled with God.

Our Food Must Be Christ

Jesus himself was the Bread of Life (John 6:35), and the one who could give them living water (John 4:10). In John 4, after he offered the woman this living water, she was so happy that she went to share this new nourishment with all of her friends! Right after she left, Jesus told the disciples (who had just returned with food) that he had already received food. When they responded in a puzzled manner, he replied that his food was to do the will of God who had sent him and to accomplish his work. He was so happy about impacting this woman's life, and so caught up in doing God's will that he literally lost his appetite!

The kind of hunger and thirst being asked of us is not that of simply enjoying a nice little meal—it suggests an all-consuming craving for a relationship with him. It is seeking him with an urgency and a feeling of being absolutely starved without him. Can you remember going without food or water for a prolonged period of time, and how you could think of little else but satisfying the cravings of your body? Jesus is telling us that we need to live in this sort of state spiritually, not that we are to go around unsatisfied, but that we will stop at nothing to continue eating and drinking of God!

The Psalmist understood well what Jesus was discussing: "As the deer pants for streams of water, so my soul pants for you, O God. My soul thirsts for God, for the living God. When can I go and meet with God?" (Psalm 42:1-2). Just how excited are you about getting time to be with God every day? Do you make time? Are you looking for more time? Is your heart yearning to be with God? Consider another passage in Psalms: "O God, you are my God, earnestly I seek you; my soul thirsts for you, my body longs for you, in a dry and weary land where there is no water…My soul will be satisfied as with the richest of foods; with singing lips my mouth will praise you" (Psalm 63:1, 5).

Not only must we be hungry in our souls for an ever-deepening walk with God, we must also be hungry and thirsty for the word of God. For a deepened conviction about loving the Word, just read through the 119th Psalm. Over and over, the writer talks of loving God's law and meditating on it day and night. He is completely delighted with it, devoid of any sense of duty in reading it (for a Quiet Time) but overjoyed at the privilege of being able to commune with the expressed heart of his Creator!

As we feast on the word of God, we will also hunger to please him, to obey him, to become more and more like him. This desire to please him will find a direct application in loving others as he does. Jesus hungered to serve others, to even give up his life for them. The things of God (Matthew 16:23) were all about serving and saving others for the glory of God. When our souls really do hunger for him, we will also hunger to bless the ones for whom Jesus died!

An Eternal Longing for Him

One of our greatest needs in growing spiritually is to keep an eternal perspective on our lives. We are not talking simply of being happy in the sense of enjoying our lives on this earth. Christianity is not another self-help approach to life or another "find yourself" philosophy. It is a religion teaching us how to live so we will know how to die. Christ is telling us how to live in our day so we will live in eternity.

My own determination to hunger and thirst for righteousness was strengthened tremendously in the past by watching a dear sister, Suzanne Atkins, face death with an amazing hunger to see God. At age 32, with two small children, she discovered that she had a serious malignancy and would die in a matter of weeks. When I went to see her in San Diego just a few days before her death, I went for the purpose of encouraging her. However, she did most of the encouraging! As the pain of cancer racked her body, her eyes were lit up with the thought of seeing the God for whom she had hungered and thirsted. Each morning when she awoke, she was disappointed that she had not yet gone to see him. As we talked and laughed and prayed and wept, the real issues of righteousness came into clear perspective. The only way to hunger to be with God in the next life is to hunger to be with him now—every day! He is not simply a part of life—he is life itself. "When Christ, who is your life, appears, then you also will appear with him in glory" (Colossians 3:4).

Suzanne left behind a family and many friends, including me, who are more determined than ever to hunger and thirst for God. My prayer is that her example of dying with the joy of Jesus will help to create a thirst in you that will lead you to live and to die as she did. If you were to die today, what would others be able to honestly say about your hungering and thirsting for God and his righteousness? When we live out the beatitude of Matthew 5:6, then we can die with the beatitude of Revelation 14:13: "Blessed are the dead who die in the Lord from now on." "Yes," says the Spirit, "they will rest from their labor, for their deeds will follow them."

QUESTIONS FOR THOUGHT

1. How intense has your hunger and thirst for righteousness been over the past several months? How do you feel about your answer?

2. Do you have a plan for Quiet Times with God and are you carrying out those plans?

3. The Bible speaks of longing to be with God in eternity. How does this idea impact your heart?

ACTION ITEMS

Select two of your Christian friends who seem to have a real hunger and thirst for God and talk with them about what inspires them.

CHAPTER TWENTY

The Bible and Peace

—Gordon Ferguson

Children love Christmas. Adults supposedly love Christmas. The Hallmark Channel definitely loves Christmas, for they begin a whole series of Christmas movies in the summer each year. Most people seem to agree with the title of the movie, "The Most Wonderful Time of the Year!" I grew up hearing one Bible verse above all others as it rang through the land—Luke 2:14: "Glory to God in the highest, and on earth, peace and good will toward men." The problem with the movie and with that passage is that for many people, it just isn't true. For a significant percentage of the population, holidays are depressing times, and the older we get, the more likely that is to be the case. Too many of our loved ones are no longer surrounding our Christmas trees.

Let's go back to that verse in Luke—its mistranslation and subsequent misapplication. Here's the real translation in the NIV (and most all modern versions): "Glory to God in the highest heaven, and on earth peace to those on whom his favor rests." Note the difference in the two translations. The passage does not say that Christmas is a time of peace and goodwill for all mankind, and reality shows that to be the case. But the Bible does say plenty about peace because God wants us to have it—but it can be only on his terms.

Without question, Jesus Christ came to bring peace, and his birth was described as a time of ushering in peace. Read the following passages with that in mind.

Isaiah 9:6

"For to us a child is born, to us a son is given, and the government will be on his shoulders. And he will be called Wonderful Counselor, Mighty God, Everlasting Father, Prince of Peace."

Isaiah 2:2-4

In the last days the mountain of the LORD's temple will be established as the highest of the mountains; it will be exalted above the hills, and all nations will stream to it. [3] Many peoples will come and say, 'Come, let us go up to the mountain of the LORD, to the temple of the God of Jacob. He will teach us his ways, so that we may walk in his paths.' The law will go out from Zion, the word of the LORD from Jerusalem. [4] He will judge between the nations and will settle disputes for many peoples. They will beat their swords into plowshares and their spears into pruning hooks. Nation will not take up sword against nation, nor will they train for war anymore."

Yet, we can say with equal certainty that Jesus Christ did *not* come to bring peace.

Matthew 10:34-39

[34] "Do not suppose that I have come to bring peace to the earth. I did not come to bring peace, but a sword. [35] For I have come to turn a man against his father, a daughter against her mother, a daughter-in-law against her mother-in-law—[36] a man's enemies will be the members of his own household. [37] Anyone who loves their father or mother more than me is not worthy of me; anyone who loves their son or daughter more than me is not worthy of me. [38] Whoever does not take up their cross and follow me is not worthy of me. [39] Whoever finds their life will lose it, and whoever loses their life for my sake will find it.

Obviously, peace is being looked at from two different vantage points, for the Bible does not contradict itself. The peace which Jesus came to bring is very different than most people would think, and it is essential that disciples of Jesus fully understand that difference. Here are two verses that will help us.

John 16:33: "I have told you these things, so that in me you may have peace. In this world you will have trouble. But take heart! I have overcome the world."

> **John 14:27:** "Peace I leave with you; my peace I give you. I do not give to you as the world gives. Do not let your hearts be troubled and do not be afraid."

What a huge chasm exists between the spiritual and the physical ideas of peace! The world seeks the peace of ease, but Christ brings the peace of struggle. The world seeks peace and prosperity, but Jesus says life consists not in the abundance of possessions (Luke 12:15). The world seeks self-gratification and satisfaction, Jesus a life of self-denial and sacrifice. The world seeks freedom from conflict, Jesus gives conflict and problems if we are fighting the spiritual battle with and for him—which will include both divine discipline (Hebrews 12) and persecution (2 Timothy 3:12).

The world will never have peace because of sin. Nations will not have peace with each other, for war is not the problem but a symptom. Humans in the world will not have peace, for Paul described relationships in the world quite bluntly but accurately in Titus 3:3 as "being hated and hating one another." Yes, we are told to pray for peace in 1 Timothy 2:1-4, but peace for a purpose (God wants all men to be saved and come to a knowledge of the truth—verse 4).

What Kind of Peace Should We Be Seeking?

First of all, peace with God, as Romans 5:1 puts it. "Therefore, since we have been justified through faith, we have peace with God through our Lord Jesus Christ." Then we should be seeking peace between races, ethnic groups, and foreigners. Ephesians 2:14-15: "For he himself is our peace, who has made the two groups one and has destroyed the barrier, the dividing wall of hostility, by setting aside in his flesh the law with its commands and regulations. His purpose was to create in himself one new humanity out of the two, thus making peace."

Next, peace between our brothers and sisters in Christ must always be a focus and a work in progress. Jesus put an amazing premium on our peace with fellow disciples. The world is to know that we are his disciples precisely because of our peace as a spiritual family.

John 13:34-35: "A new command I give you: Love one another. As I have loved you, so you must love one another. [35] By this everyone will know that you are my disciples, if you love one another."

John 17:20-21: "My prayer is not for them alone. I pray also for those who will believe in me through their message, [21] that all of them may be one, Father, just as you are in me and I am in you. May they also be in us so that the world may believe that you have sent me."

Further, our goal is to be at peace with all people, at least as far as we can control and influence it.

Romans 12:17-21: Do not repay anyone evil for evil. Be careful to do what is right in the eyes of everyone. [18] If it is possible, as far as it depends on you, live at peace with everyone. [19] Do not take revenge, my dear friends, but leave room for God's wrath, for it is written: 'It is mine to avenge; I will repay,' says the Lord. [20] On the contrary: 'If your enemy is hungry, feed him; if he is thirsty, give him something to drink. In doing this, you will heap burning coals on his head.' [21] Do not be overcome by evil, but overcome evil with good."

Finally, we are to seek peace of mind, which only God can give when we follow his principles for finding it. Philippians 4:6-7: "Do not be anxious about anything, but in every situation, by prayer and petition, with thanksgiving, present your requests to God. [7] And the peace of God, which transcends all understanding, will guard your hearts and your minds in Christ Jesus." God's cure for anxiety is found by offering all kinds of prayers, including thanksgiving. How does thanksgiving alleviate anxiety? It forces you to go back in your life and look at the times God blessed you and delivered you from other anxiety-filled times. In this case, the key to the future is the past. If God has brought you through past challenges, you can trust him to do it again.

Don't be fooled about the kinds of peace the world is going to experience (or not experience), and don't miss out on these four kinds that God is offering us. There is peace that transcends all understanding, and it is a combination of the types of peace that Jesus came to bring. Receive Jesus' peace thankfully!

QUESTIONS FOR THOUGHT

1. Which of the four kinds of peace described are the most difficult for you to envision finding and maintaining? Why?

2. How would you rank your level of peace in each of those four areas?

3. What can you imagine doing that would make these types of peace stronger in your mind and stronger in your emotions?

ACTION ITEMS

Write an evaluation of each of the four types of peace as you believe they exist in your life now. List at least one thing you can do to strengthen peace in each area and then share them with a spiritual friend and start praying about implementing your plans.

CHAPTER TWENTY-ONE

Reclaiming the Glory of God
Part 1: Losing the Glory of God

—Gordon Ferguson

"There is no difference between Jew and Gentile, for all have
sinned and fall short of the glory of God..." (Romans 3:23)

The original pair were highly blessed at their creation, having
been made in the very image of God himself (Genesis 1:26-27).
They shared in God's nature and glory. However, Adam and Eve
chose to reject their exalted position by sinning. Sadly, we all have
chosen to do exactly the same thing, "for all have sinned and fall
short of the glory of God" (Romans 3:23).

To assist us in our rejection of God's glory is our highly intel-
ligent and effective enemy—Satan. His use of temptations in our
lives is powerful. If we are to reclaim the glory of God, we must be
totally familiar with his tactics. As Paul put it, "...in order that Satan
might not outwit us. For we are not unaware of his schemes" (2 Corinthians 2:11). Sin must be identified and understood to be defeated.
A disciple's defenses cannot afford to be weakened through igno-
rance or naivety. Two areas that we need to perceive more clearly
regarding sin are its insidiousness and deceitfulness.

Temptations Never Stop Coming

The temptation to sin is insidious. Satan's attacks are constant. James tells us to "Resist the devil, and he will flee from
you" (James 4:7). Yet, he only leaves until there is an opportune
time to return (Luke 4:13). There is no vacation from Satan. Peter
reminds us of the nature of Satan: "Be alert and of sober mind.
Your enemy the devil prowls around like a roaring lion looking for

someone to devour" (1 Peter 5: 8). We must always be on guard against his clever designs to destroy us. Not only are his attacks constant—they also focus on our weakest points. In fact, in Paul's letter to the Christians in Rome, he discusses the power and effect of sin more than in any book in the Bible. Here are just a few of the many scriptures:

Romans 3:9
"...For we have already made the charge that Jews and Gentile alike are all under the power of sin."

Romans 5:12
"Therefore, just as sin entered the world through one man, and death through sin, and in this way death came to all people, because all sinned."

Romans 6:12-13
"Therefore do not let sin reign in your mortal body so that you obey its evil desires. Do not offer any part of yourself to sin as an instrument of wickedness..."

Romans 6:23
"For the wages of sin is death, but the gift of God is eternal life in Christ Jesus our Lord."

Romans 8:10
"But if Christ is in you, then even though your body is subject to death because of sin, the Spirit gives life because of righteousness."

Some of our weaknesses are a result of background influences as children over which we had no control. Most of our weaknesses resulted from our own choice to sin repeatedly. We may remain weak, even as Christians, because the fellowship we are a part of is weak, and real openness is not encouraged nor practiced. The Apostle John reminds us: "If we confess our sins, he is faithful and just and will forgive us our sins and purify us from all unrighteousness" (1 John 1:9). Without exposure of sin to the light through confession, it cannot be overcome. John made this principle abundantly clear in his Gospel.

John 3:19-21

> [19] This is the verdict: Light has come into the world, but people loved darkness instead of light because their deeds were evil. [20] Everyone who does evil hates the light, and will not come into the light for fear that their deeds will be exposed. [21] But whoever lives by the truth comes into the light, so that it may be seen plainly that what they have done has been done in the sight of God.

Satan also attacks us at unexpected points. Even after years of being strong in an area of our lives, we can suddenly find ourselves falling in that very area. Sometimes we are aided in falling when encouraged to sin by an unexpected source—a close friend or family member. Peter was called "Satan" when he tried to steer his friend, Jesus, away from the cross (Matthew 16:21-23). Our closest friends become temporary enemies when they try to keep us from self-denial. Some of the worst sins we commit are likely in the category of omission, like not sharing our faith, not helping the poor, or not confessing our sins (James 4:17).

Satan is the Master of Deceit

The temptation to sin is deceitful. Satan is amazing in his subtlety. We often are blind to our sins. We are easily self-deceived. We may see the sins of others quite clearly but miss an entire "plank" in our own eye (Matthew 7:4). This blindness keeps us in sin. Jesus was unapologetic in his attitude about this area. In the Sermon on the Mount, he says: "You hypocrite, first take the plank out of your own eye, and then you will see clearly to remove the speck from your brother's eyes." (Matthew 7:5). The only way to overcome such deception is to have constant input from those who know us. Ask for it; don't wait for it!

Sin is also deceitful in that we become desensitized to it. The Hebrew writer had to point out that even believers can be "...hardened by sin's deceitfulness" (Hebrews 3:13), and "can abandon the faith and follow deceiving spirits and things taught by demons. Such teachings come through hypocritical liars, whose consciences have been seared as with a hot iron" (1 Timothy 4:1-2). A person can be insensitive to sin due to having a wrong definition of it. To him it may only be doing bad things, when failing to do good things can be much worse (James 4:17). Jesus warns about this deception in one of the most sobering passages in the New Testament. He described a segment of people who claimed to be disciples but had been deceived by sin. Jesus says to them:

Matthew 7:21-23

[21] "Not everyone who says to me, 'Lord, Lord,' will enter the kingdom of heaven, but only the one who does the will of my Father who is in heaven. [22] Many will say to me on that day, 'Lord, Lord, did we not prophesy in your name and in your name drive out demons and in your name perform many miracles?' [23] Then I will tell them plainly, 'I never knew you. Away from me, you evildoers!'

We can be deceived by sin when we plan to change or act later. Procrastination is one of Satan's finest tools. The way to hell truly can be paved with good intentions. We may tell ourselves that we are meditating on our condition, or figuring out the best course to pursue in changing, but the fact remains that we are failing to do what we know is right. Waiting is not indecision. It is absolutely a decision to refuse to follow convictions. The lag time between knowing and doing is a measure of disobedience.

Sin is not only deceitful in the way it attacks us—it turns us into deceivers. Deceitfulness can become part of our character, as we can go "…from bad to worse, deceiving and being deceived" (2 Timothy 3:13). This malady may surface in subtle forms like rationalization, but if unchecked, it will lead to overt lying. We must be convicted that half-truths are untruths. We are either totally honest, or we are dishonest. It is time to be black-and-white in our view of sin. A "gray view" of ourselves is harmful because it delays or prohibits repentance. When we sin, we fail to reflect the glory God has designed for us. Sin is both deceitful and highly insidious. Like a gas seeking an entrance into an empty compartment, sin seeks an entrance into a compartment intended only for the Spirit of God. Satan remains that roaring lion who constantly seeks to devour us (1 Peter 5:8). We must resist him exactly as the Lord directs us. The next chapter will focus on how to regain that glory which has been tarnished by sin.

QUESTIONS FOR THOUGHT

1. Have you let down your guard in your battle with sin? Do you confess your sins to others like you did when you were a new believer?

2. What are some of the areas of your life that Satan is attacking to weaken or destroy your faith?

3. What sins in your life are you most likely to be self-deceived about?

ACTION ITEMS

Make a list of sins in which you feel you are most vulnerable to Satan's attacks. Share this with friends to whom you have made yourself accountable.

CHAPTER TWENTY-TWO

Reclaiming the Glory of God
Part 2: Regaining the Glory

—Gordon Ferguson

"Examine yourselves to see whether you are in the faith; test yourselves. Do you not realize that Christ Jesus is in you—unless, of course, you fail the test? And I trust that you will discover that you have not failed the test." (2 Corinthians 13:5-6)

In the previous chapter about reclaiming God's glory, we discussed "losing the glory." That loss was caused exclusively by sin, which was shown to be highly insidious and deceitful. In this chapter, the focus will be on how it is possible to regain the glory lost by sin.

Praise God that he has offered us the possibility of new life and the power to continually change and mature! However, the cure is radical because the malady is both powerful and devastating. God's cure is a radical reclamation project in several ways.

One, it required God to become man. That is radical! Even more radical is the fact that he then went to a cross to suffer for our sins. Paul explained this to the Christians in Rome: "You see, at just the right time, when we were still powerless, Christ died for the ungodly. Very rarely will anyone die for a righteous person, though for a good person someone might possibly dare to die. But God demonstrates his own love for us in this: While we were still sinners, Christ died for us" (Romans 5:6-8). This means that Deity died on that cross. God died in the person of Jesus Christ as the only solution to our sin problem. How grievous sin must be! How great God's love must be (1 John 3:1)!

Two, the cure for sin is radical because it demands that we

ruthlessly attack our own sinful natures. We must be honest to the core about our motives, our attitudes, and every other aspect of our heart system. Rationalization must end. Our view of sin as "little misdemeanors" must cease, for they are the roots that grow into the more obvious sins. Anything that weakens us must be avoided. Sin is a plague, and we must treat it as such. Openness at the temptation level is necessary. We must come fully into the light, not just into its edges. The Apostle John helps make this clear in a passage worth reading a second time: "This is the verdict: Light has come into the world, but people loved darkness instead of light because their deeds were evil. Everyone who does evil hates the light, and will not come into the light for fear that their deeds will be exposed. But whoever lives by the truth comes into the light, so that it may be seen plainly that what they have done has been done in the sight of God" (John 3:19-21).

Confession is not simply good for the soul, as the old saying puts it, but it is essential to being cleansed by God's forgiveness (1 John 1:9). For complete spiritual and emotional healing, sin must be confessed to other people (James 5:16). And the quicker we confess at the very beginnings of temptation, the more Satan is blocked from our hearts. We must remain ready to eradicate temptation and sin from our lives no matter what the cost. Matthew 18:8-9 puts it this way: "If your hand or your foot causes you to stumble, cut it off and throw it away. It is better for you to enter life maimed or crippled than to have two hands or two feet and be thrown into eternal fire. [9] And if your eye causes you to stumble, gouge it out and throw it away. It is better for you to enter life with one eye than to have two eyes and be thrown into the fire of hell." Now that is radical! Not only must we deal with sin in this manner, but we must also be willing to apply the same treatment to our priority system in life. There is a time to evaluate (every day); a time to regulate (when something besides Jesus is becoming too important in our values); and a time to amputate (when the regulation does not stop the problem). Sin, in any form and at any level, must be ruthlessly attacked. That was the point that Paul was making to the believers in Colossae:

Colossians 3:5-10

> [5] Put to death, therefore, whatever belongs to your earthly nature: sexual immorality, impurity, lust, evil desires and greed, which is idolatry. [6] Because of these, the wrath of God is coming. [7] You used to walk in these ways, in the life you once lived. [8] But now you must also rid yourselves of all such things as these: anger, rage, malice, slander, and filthy language from your lips. [9] Do not lie to each other, since you have taken off your old self with its practices [10] and have put on the new self, which is being renewed in knowledge in the image of its Creator.

Three, the cure for sin is radical because it necessitates a "take-nothing-for-granted" approach to discipleship. The cardinal rule for discipling another person is to assume nothing. Any person can become guilty of any sin at any time. Therefore, we must be very perceptive and very realistic without becoming suspicious and cynical. That balance is truly a God-given balance. We will never achieve it without much prayer and strong guidance of the Holy Spirit. Practically speaking, we must watch for little indications that our spiritual friends may be weakening or struggling with temptations. "Playing our hunches" will be necessary in the sense of checking things out that we are sensing, without being accusatory.

By all means, we must learn to ask probing questions. If we are striving to be Christ-like in every way, questions do not bother us, because we understand the necessity of being asked. As surely as we understand the need of questioning by a physician regarding our physical condition, we should understand the same need concerning our spiritual condition. We must always stand ready to give others in-depth spiritual "check-ups" and be ready to submit to the same as we are discipled to be like Christ (2 Corinthians 13:5-6).

Four, the cure for sin is radical because it affects the entire church. We not only watch for sin in ourselves and in those with whom we have a discipling relationship, but we watch with concern for every other disciple. While we are not "speck inspectors" (Matthew 7:3), we are "fruit inspectors" (Matthew 7:16-20). Love demands that we be our brother's keeper with a willingness to get involved (Matthew 18:15-17; Galatians 6:1-2).

Another way that the entire church gets involved is through group confession and repentance. Numerous times in the Old Testament a large segment of the nation, or even the entire nation, was called to group repentance. Similarly, John the Baptist understood the need for this dynamic (Matthew 3:5-8). The early church also practiced the same thing (Acts 19:18-20). Opportunities for group repentance and repentance within the presence of a group are sorely needed. Yes, the cure for sin is radical, but the results of the cure provide "times of refreshing" from the Lord (Acts 3:19).

QUESTIONS FOR THOUGHT

1. The Scriptures make it clear that Jesus (God) took the form of a man and humbled himself to the point of sacrificing his life (Philippians 2:5-8). How does that motivate you to follow him?

2. Would you consider yourself radical in dealing with your sins? If so, what have you done which demonstrates that?

3. 2 Corinthians 13:5-6 says we need to examine ourselves to see if Christ is in us. When was the last time you did that?

ACTION ITEMS

Ask your spouse or your closest friends: Are there areas in my life that are not Christlike? With that feedback make radical decisions to change and deal with sin to become more Christlike.

CHAPTER TWENTY-THREE

Reclaiming the Glory of God
Part 3: Increasing the Glory

—Gordon Ferguson

"And we all, who with unveiled faces contemplate the Lord's glory, are being transformed into his image with ever-increasing glory, which comes from the Lord, who is the Spirit." (2 Corinthians 3:18)

In our previous two segments of examining this topic, we discussed how mankind lost the glory of God and then how it can be regained. This final segment will focus on increasing the glory of God in our lives on a daily basis. Without question, that increase is both desired by the Lord and made possible by his grace.

The godly qualities listed in 2 Peter 1:5-7 are essential to an effective Christian life: "For this very reason, make every effort to add to your faith goodness; and to goodness, knowledge; and to knowledge, self-control; and to self-control, perseverance; and to perseverance, godliness; and to godliness, mutual affection; and to mutual affection, love. For if you possess these qualities in increasing measure, they will keep you from being ineffective and unproductive in your knowledge of our Lord Jesus Christ." Especially take note of verse 7—"if you possess these qualities in *increasing* measure."

The Christian life is not static; there is growth, change and increase! Paul shares the same sentiment with the Corinthians: "Though outwardly we are wasting away, yet inwardly we are being renewed day by day" (2 Corinthians 4:16). Earlier in the letter he talks about how we should reflect God's glory in these words: "And we all, who with unveiled faces contemplate the Lord's glory, are being transformed into his image with ever-increasing glory, which comes from the Lord, who is the Spirit" (2 Corinthians 3:18). This ever-increasing glory in our lives provides us with some marvelous benefits.

Continual Freedom from Sin's Guilt

This release from the guilt of sin (and a guilty conscience) provides the relief which frees us up to keep growing. As we walk in the light, "…we have fellowship with one another, and the blood of Jesus, his Son, purifies us from all sin" (1 John 1:7). The verb "purifies" is present tense in the Greek, signifying a continued cleansing. Just as windshield wipers on a car continually remove the rain, the blood of Jesus continually takes away our sin. In our physical body, our blood is constantly flowing, and impurities are being removed from it. In Christ's spiritual body, the church, his blood is constantly removing spiritual impurities. This purifying is contingent on our "walking in the light."

This walk is just that—a walk with God. It is not a sinless walk, or else there would be no sin from which to be purified. But it is a faithful walk made possible by a heart devoted completely to God, coupled with a life which consistently reflects that devotion. In Christian marriages, there are no perfect mates, but praise God there are many faithful ones. This illustration helps us to see that God accepts faithfulness from those in Christ in lieu of the perfection which we cannot attain. When our fellowship with God is constant, we are freed up to grow into the image of Christ in that ever-increasing measure.

Great Relationships with Others

As we become more like God, we are enabled to love like he did. We must remember "God's love has been poured out into our hearts through the Holy Spirit, who has been given to us" (Romans 5:5). As a result, "Now that you have purified yourselves by obeying the truth so that you have sincere love for each other, love one another deeply, from the heart" (1 Peter 1:22). For those in Christ, love is an increasing reality. This explains why there should be no divorces in marriages of true disciples. They get closer and closer to God and therefore to each other as well. Picture each spouse at the bottom two angles of a triangle and God at the top. As the couple gets closer to God, they also get closer to one another. This reality also explains why the kingdom of God should be characterized by unity in Christ. When we consider others better than ourselves (Philippians 2:3), unity is assured. And then the lofty ideas found in Christ's prayer of John 17:20-23 are practically realized rather than just being paid lip service.

The one quality of love in Christ that stands in stark contrast to love in the world is its unconditional nature. God's acceptance of us in Christ regardless of our weaknesses frees us to mature from those weaknesses. Our acceptance of one another despite imperfections provides the encouragement we need to keep growing in our service to God and to others. In worldly relationships, problems which come up often destroy the relationships rather quickly. In godly relationships, problems lead to spiritual confrontation, reconciliation, and growth (Matthew 5:24). Praise the Lord that we can love each other in an ever-increasing measure as we imitate him.

A New Relationship with Ourselves

We can actually accept ourselves and love ourselves in the right way. That is why Jesus said, "Love your neighbor as yourself" (Matthew 22:39). You'll have a difficult time loving your neighbor if you don't have the proper love for yourself. People in the world are often uncomfortable with who they are. Their insides are not together. But in Jesus, we can be comfortable with who we are in him and with what we are becoming. We accept ourselves as God and other disciples do, in order that we can be freed up from self-condemnation and really grow.

Being down on ourselves is not spiritual. It is devilish and crippling. This is the message that Paul was teaching the Thessalonians. He told them: "May the Lord make your love increase and overflow for each other and for everyone else, just as ours does for you" (1 Thessalonians 3:12). This is the key to tremendous spiritual growth and a witness that we belong to Jesus. Remember the words Jesus told his disciples after he washed their dirty feet: "A new command I give you: Love one another. As I have loved you, so you must love one another. By this everyone will know that you are my disciples, if you love one another" (John 13:34-35).

As we reclaim that glory which God offers, let us set our sights high. We are made in the image of God and remade in Christ's image. Let us live like it: "This is how we know we are in him: Whoever claims to live in him must live as Jesus did" (1 John 2:5-6).

QUESTIONS FOR THOUGHT

1. Of all the Christian qualities listed in 2 Peter 1:5-7, which is your greatest strength, and which one do you need to work on the most?

2. 1 Peter 1:22 reminds us that obeying the truth has a purifying effect. Do you have a daily mindset of obedience to God? Is it resulting in being able to love others deeply?

3. Do you have a proper love for yourself or a negative view of your life?

ACTION ITEMS

We are called to make every effort to reflect God with an ever-increasing glory. Ask your closest spiritual friend this week what areas of your life need to be worked on to reflect God in a greater way.

CHAPTER TWENTY-FOUR

Falling in Love with God Again

—Theresa Ferguson

The title represents an important principle: we can lose our first love for God. Jesus raised this issue with the Laodicean church in Revelation 2:4: "Yet I hold this against you: You have forsaken the love you had at first." Our love for God and for people cannot remain static. Either it is growing, or it begins to diminish. When it does the latter, it is time to go back to the basics, and that should lead us to what Jesus called the greatest command of all. When he was asked what this command was, his reply is found in Matthew 22:37-38.

> Jesus replied: "Love the Lord your God with all your heart and with all your soul and with all your mind. [38] This is the first and greatest commandment."

It is encouraging to note that even though people were testing Jesus, he still went straight for the heart – using a passage that they loved and held in highest regard. Without doubt, Jesus wants to go directly at our hearts right now.

Love God with All Your *Mind*

True love always begins in the mind before it reaches down to the heart, for our thinking determines our emotions. God has given us a love letter, the Bible, so that our minds can always remember how much God loves us, no matter what we may be going through.

These days, you can find letters as though from God online that piece together his many statements from various passages describing his love for you. You would do well to locate one of those (or ask me for one) and read it often. We too easily forget how many such affirmations of God's love for us are found in Scripture.

I don't know how reading such sentiments from God makes you feel, but they convince me that he really wants a deeper relationship with me. Although he knows everything about me—the good and the bad—he still deeply desires to have a personal relationship with me. Amazing! Amazing Grace—how sweet the sound!

We need to use our minds to remember. To remember who God is—he is love; and any love that exists in this world is there because of who he is (1 John 4:8). He is my loving Creator, my loving Judge, and my loving Father. We can feel that when we are struggling spiritually, God somehow turns his back on us until we are doing better. But think about if that works with you and your children or other loved ones. When they are not doing well, that is when our hearts go out to them the most! Keep reminding yourself of who God really is and of the promises he has given us. God is good—only good—and always works everything out for our good (Romans 8:28).

Love God with All Your Heart

After Jesus rebuked the church in Laodicea for losing their first love, he admonished them to repent at a heart level. "Consider how far you have fallen! Repent and do the things you did at first. If you do not repent, I will come to you and remove your lampstand from its place" (Revelation 2:5). When you examine the commendations this church received, then you understand that doing the things we did at first has much more to do with the heart than with the actions. It is not about working, or even working hard—it is about our heart being like it was when we first became Christians. This doesn't mean that we don't keep working, but it does mean that we keep working on our hearts. We cannot focus only on our actions; we must put equal or greater focus on our hearts at the same time.

If you are married, think back to when you first fell in love with your spouse and ask yourself this question: How did you feel when you thought about him or her? How did you feel as a new Christian when you thought about Jesus? That is what God is after today: our hearts falling in love with him again! What makes our hearts draw nearer to God? More than anything else, our gratitude. Think back to how you felt when you came up from the waters of baptism. What a relief! What a burden was lifted! What an amazing God allowing you to experience such joy for your salvation!

What will get that feeling back? Thinking and praying through all your blessings and thinking about what your life might be like if you had not become a Christian. Just think of how he shows his love to us. One of the books that helped our marriage was *The 5 Love Languages* by Gary Chapman. Reading that book and discussing it together a chapter at a time rekindled our love for one another, when frankly, it had grown stale. Apply this concept to God, and you will see that he shows his love abundantly in all five of the ways described in that book.

1. Gifts given to you – Jesus, for starters!

2. Touch – he reaches out to touch us in different ways, but the obvious way is through those whom he has placed in our lives.

3. Words of affirmation – the Bible is absolutely full of these, especially seen in God's promises.

4. Acts of service – need we say more than to simply look at his innumerable acts of kindness shown to us in our lifetimes?

5. Quality time – He longs to talk to us, even giving us his phone number, and he always picks up! **JER-333** (Jeremiah 33:3—"Call to me and I will answer you and tell you great and unsearchable things you do not know.")

Just like in a marriage relationship, when the closeness is not there, you do whatever it takes to get the hearts rekindled. As the old hymn puts it, we just need to count our blessings and name them one by one!

Love God with All of Your *Soul*

Our soul is that inner part of us made in God's image, and it will survive with God forever. Remember that we are made in God's image to enjoy a relationship with him and to show others this image drawing them to God as well. Remember the sacrifice that God made to save our souls. We need to keep asking ourselves the question of why he did this, and the only answer is simple, but unbelievably profound: because he loved us so. The blood poured out at the cross still works spiritually to continually cleanse us of our sins (1 John 1:7). This cleansing is a continual action verb. As we walk in the light (which does not mean sinless perfection on our parts), we are continually cleansed.

How does falling in love again with God cause us to become more and more like him? Because of his love and sacrifice, we now view people as he does. We see those who are hurting, and our hearts go out to them. We see those who are lost and share the gospel with them, as one beggar who has found bread shares it with other hungry folks. We see those who are confused—in and out of the church and our patient reassurance goes out to them. We see those who are angry and hurt, and we show them the way of forgiveness. We see those who are questioning God's love, and we help them to surrender once more.

As we are falling in love with God again and again with our mind, heart and soul, our impact upon others is multiplied. We want our spouses and children and grandchildren to love God with all of their being—and through our example and our love, we can help them do that. We want our families and friends to be saved —and with God using us as vessels, that can become a reality. As an older woman wanting so much to pass on my heart for God to you, these words provide a fitting conclusion to this chapter: "Even when I am old and gray, do not forsake me, O God, till I declare your power to the next generation, your might to all who are to come" (Psalm 71:18).

QUESTIONS FOR THOUGHT

1. In considering what your first love for Christ was like, how would you describe it now in comparison?

2. What do you think loving God with all your mind, heart, and soul boils down to in practical terms? Explain why.

3. Which thoughts or illustrations from this chapter hit your heart most and how can you apply them best?

ACTION ITEMS

Read through the chapter a couple of times and make note of the practical steps you can take to increase your love for Jesus. Then write out an action plan for daily use.

CHAPTER TWENTY-FIVE

Faith that Pleases God, Part 1

—Theresa Ferguson

"And without faith it is impossible to please God, because any-one who comes to him must believe that he exists and that he rewards those who earnestly seek him." (Hebrews 11:6)

All of us have a working definition of faith in our minds, but the multitude of events in my 81 years of life have forced me back to the drawing table to take a deeper look at faith time and time again. My earlier faith had to grow to meet the challenges of my life as it has unfolded. The greatest desire of my heart is to please God. Yet in my sinful nature, I am a people pleaser. Over the years, I have learned to focus on what really pleases God, which is to have faith in his work in my life in all circumstances. I have learned to face the facts, and then *faith* the facts—not to *fake* the facts or to *fret* the facts.

Faith Must Be Tested

In other words, I have learned to face the facts with faith, and not stay stuck in the fears and feelings of the past. Consequently, when someone asks me if my faith is stronger or weaker after fac-ing a challenge, I can truthfully say that my faith in God is much stronger than in the past. Why? Because my faith has been seri-ously tested, like that of everyone else trying to please God, yet I have decided to believe, trust, and obey the principles of Hebrews 11:6 daily. This has long been one of my theme Scriptures, along with several others such as Matthew 22:37-40, 1 Thessalonians 5:16-20 and Philippians 4:4-9.

One principle will always be true: only a tested faith will be a growing faith. Major events have occurred in my life through the years to provide those tests. I have experienced the deaths of all four of our parents, along with the loss of my oldest brother. Significant changes have occurred in our church culture, and many relationships in our movement of churches were lost or distanced due to moving from one city to another through the years. Challenges in my family have added to the testing process. As a result, I have gone through the stages of grief and loss: shock and denial; anger; guilt; deep sadness; and through it all, learning to trust God at a deeper level than ever before.

In the terms of Psalm 18:16, "He reached down from on high and took hold of me; he drew me out of deep waters." I felt like Jesus came down into the deep with me and led me out. I have learned that faith is not faith unless it is tested. I have been hanging on to God as he has hung on to me, and in the process, been helping others to work through their struggles by reminding them of the following Scriptures and practical applications of them.

A Comprehensive Definition of Faith

Hebrews 11:6 provides us with the best, brief definition of faith to be found in the entire Bible. It contains a three-part definition. First, we must believe that God exists. For most of us, that is not a challenge. Romans 1:20 states it well, claiming that God's invisible qualities are clearly seen through his creation of the universe. As we saw our children born, and years later, our grandchildren born, their creation shouted loudly that God indeed exists.

Second, Hebrews 11:6 says we must believe that God rewards us—which is where our challenge deepens. Has God rewarded you the way you believe he should? Has he treated you the way you believe you should be treated? Some of us think that God is doing his part, but somehow man has blocked God's desire to do us good—men have messed up God's plan to reward and bless us! That kind of thinking shows we have a very shallow and erroneous view of God.

What do the Scriptures say about God's power and plans to direct the affairs of mankind? Isaiah 45:7: "I form the light and create darkness, I bring prosperity and create disaster; I, the Lord, do all these things." Lamentations 3:37-38: "Who can speak and have it happen if the Lord has not decreed it? Is it not from the mouth of the Most High that both calamities and good things come?" Job

2:10 "Shall we accept good from God, and not trouble?" These passages make it clear that our faith must grow considerably so the deeper challenges of life will not unsettle our faith in God's absolute control of our lives. God either causes or allows everything that happens to occur, and our faith has to be big enough to encompass this reality.

Third, our passage says that God rewards those who earnestly seek him. How do we earnestly seek him? Two biblical concepts stand out in this regard. We must seek him with our whole hearts, and we must seek him with absolute perseverance. For the first concept, see the following verses: Jeremiah 29:11-13; 1 Chronicles 28:9; and 2 Chronicles 16:9. This last one reads: "For the eyes of the Lord range throughout the earth to strengthen those whose hearts are fully committed to him." For the second concept, perseverance, see these verses: Romans 2:6-7; Gal. 6:9; Eph. 6:13; 2 Thess. 3:13; Hebrews 3:14; 12:1-2, 11-13, 15; and James 1:12.

Examples of Faith that Pleased God

Many, many examples can be given of those who wrestled with God and refused to give up on his hand working powerfully in their lives. Some of the most impressive are found in the text of Hebrews 11. Noah, in Hebrews 11:7, is a good one with which to begin. Genesis 6:3 seems to imply that the ark was in preparation for 120 years. To Noah's neighbors looking on, the idea of a flood seemed preposterous. Imagine the ridicule he faced, and the perseverance involved in facing it, but he had a faith that pleased God, and he got his reward: he saved himself and his family.

Next, in Hebrews 11:8-19, Abraham is introduced as a man who moved hundreds of miles from his homeland, with neither a travel plan nor a life plan. But he maintained his faith. Why? He and his family were focused on a reward in heaven, not on earth. God then made him wait a long time for the birth of Isaac, again a promise to bless but without a plan. Finally, the ultimate test was being told to sacrifice that son of promise. Through all of this, he simply had to trust God despite some challenging circumstances. God's hand in our lives often doesn't make sense, and it tests our faith to the nth degree!

Joseph (Hebrews 11:22) had to face amazingly difficult tests even as a very young man. He was sold into slavery by his own brothers (most of whom wanted to kill him). For refusing to be immoral, he was thrown into jail. Next, he was forgotten by the butler of Pharaoh, whom he had served, and after 13 long years, he ended up second-in-command of Egypt!

In Hebrews 11:23-27, we find the amazing story of how Moses was raised as Pharaoh's son. Imagine what Moses might have become in a worldly sense had he not exercised faith in the God of his fathers. When he decided it was time for God to use him, he killed an Egyptian, which resulted in him spending the next 40 years in the desert. He had his plan of what he thought his life should be, but God had quite another. What was his faith like? He persevered for those 40 years and ended up doing the bidding of God in forming the nation of Israel. He put up with the faithless people of God who were quite unappreciative of all that he did. He served God tirelessly in the wilderness and was blocked from entering into the promised land—yet he did not waver in his faithfulness to God. The real training by God occurs when we refuse to quit trusting and obeying him even when the going gets rough.

QUESTIONS FOR THOUGHT

1. In looking at the definition of faith in Hebrews 11, where is your faith strongest and weakest?

2. Which of the examples of faith in Hebrews 11 resonates with you the most, and why?

3. Since faith grows by being tested, what were some of your greatest periods of spiritual testing? Explain the effects upon your faith.

ACTION ITEMS

The testing of our faith often produces real challenges, even traumatic ones. Ultimately the tests can serve as steppingstones to greater faith or stumbling blocks to damage our faith. Make a list of both types in your life and discuss it with a trusted spiritual friend.

CHAPTER TWENTY-SIX

Faith that Pleases God, Part 2

—Theresa Ferguson

"And without faith it is impossible to please God, because anyone who comes to him must believe that he exists and that
he rewards those who earnestly seek him." (Hebrews 11:6)

In Part 1, we examined Hebrews 11:6 as a brief but compre-
hensive definition of faith which pleases God. We studied the
principle of faith growing mostly through its testing, and the more
challenging the test, the greater the growth. As the weightlifters
say, "No pain, no gain." But we also considered the possibility
that challenges can be traumatic and can damage our faith if we
don't handle them with faith. The same events can either be steppingstones to greater faith or stumbling blocks in our faith journey. Then we looked at some of the Bible's greatest examples of
faith as recorded in Hebrews 11, all of whom faced overwhelming
challenges but met them with a faith that persevered. The focus
of Part 2 is on how we can increase our faith in the midst of our
challenges.

Lord, Increase Our Faith!

The need for a strong, growing faith is obvious − but how do
we increase it when we are weak and hurting spiritually? Here are
some biblical steps that are very practical. First, make a decision.
A common mistake of those who preach and teach is to demand
faith without helping to build it. Just saying, "You need more
faith" is not helpful. We need help in building it, but surprisingly,
this help begins by deciding to see our faith grow. Repenting may
be the very means to gaining faith in the first place. Consider these
verses in that light. "Repent and believe the good news" (Mark

1:15). If you keep doubting your beliefs, you will end up believing your doubts! Other key verses are Mark 5:36—"Don't be afraid; just believe" and John 20:27—"Stop doubting and believe." I have prayed all night several times to get deeper convictions about repenting of certain things. Making significant decisions can be emotionally challenging, especially spiritual decisions that we realize carry responsibilities for change.

Next, pray for faith. Note the prayer of the father whose son was demon possessed in Mark 9:22b-24: "But if you can do anything, take pity on us and help us." 23 'If you can'?" said Jesus. 'Everything is possible for one who believes.' 24 Immediately the boy's father exclaimed, 'I do believe; help me overcome my unbelief!'" The conversation sheds some light on both the need for and the power of faith. Pay close attention to the prayer of the father, and the implication given to the disciples when they couldn't cast out the demon. They too had the problem of a lack of faith. Similarly, in Luke 17, Jesus informed his disciples they must forgive those who sin against them an unlimited number of times, after which they pled: "Increase our faith (Luke 17:5)."

As we continue to read Luke 17, we see humility is a necessary ingredient for God to increase our faith. When we are humble, we readily admit our need for more faith and easily ask God for it. Additionally, we must pray for perseverance and wholeheartedness—two indispensable qualities needed to build our faith. Philippians 4:6-7 provides us with another key to a type of prayer that builds faith, the prayer of thanksgiving as we surrender our anxiety. Why do you think unloading anxiety is aided by thanksgiving? Because it makes us focus on God's blessings in the past, reassuring us that if he blessed us in the past, he will now. If he delivered us from the things in life that caused our anxiety, he will deliver us now. Thus, the key to the future is actually the past, for God's goodness is not in short supply.

Third, camp out in the word of God. Romans 10:17 and Romans 15:4 make important promises regarding how Scripture builds faith. The first reads: "Consequently, faith comes from hearing the message, and the message is heard through the word about Christ." The second reads: "For everything that was written in the past was written to teach us, so that through endurance and the encouragement of the Scriptures we might have hope." Study the promises of God, such as Psalm 37:25: "I was young and now I am old, yet I have never seen the righteous forsaken or their children begging bread." 1 Corinthians 10:13 gives us a precious promise of protection: "No temptation has seized you except what is common to man. And God is faithful; he will not let you be tempted beyond what you can bear. But when you are tempted, he will also provide a way out so that you can stand up under it." Romans 8:28 through the end of the chapter is another favorite of mine. Read about God's heroes of the Old Testament, and above all, read about the life of Jesus in the Gospel accounts – his treatment of saints and sinners. Reading spiritual books and listening to recorded sermons also help us to build faith through the Word they expound upon.

Fourth, borrow faith from those who have more than you. People were attracted to Jesus in droves in part because he exuded faith. Philippians 4:9 instructs us to get around positive, faithful people. "Whatever you have learned or received or heard from me or seen in me—put it into practice. And the God of peace will be with you." Being around some people just leaves you feeling good and feeling hopeful. Being around other people makes you feel just the opposite, so choose your friends well. And decide to be (or become) a positive person yourself, as Philippians 4:8 teaches us. To encourage is to "put courage into." One of the most important things we need to restore in our fellowship is that of encouraging one another with the Bible.

Finally, put your faith to the test. This is exactly what Peter did in Luke 5:1-11. I often begin a new year by challenging my faith in this way: I list the three hardest things to believe can happen in my life. I then write out Scriptures that inspire me to believe they can happen with God's help. Next, I write out a plan to help me see these things become a reality. Lastly, I decide to have the faith the size of a mustard seed—Matthew 17:20: "I tell you the truth, if you have faith as small as a mustard seed, you can say to this mountain, 'Move from here to there' and it will move. Nothing will be impossible for you." Don't wait until you feel like it to start doing what you know you should. Obey and pray for more faith as you go. This principle has always worked for me. Some pull back in unbelief, and say to God, "give me faith and I will do right again;" but God is saying, "Do right again and I will give you faith!" May he help all who read this to increase their faith by following God's principles, and to enjoy the abundant blessings that result from a faith that pleases God!

QUESTIONS FOR THOUGHT

1. Do you think that making a decision to have faith in a certain area and then acting on that decision is difficult or easy? Give it a try.

2. Although the old hymn directs us to "trust and obey," why do you think Jesus often reversed those steps – obey and trust?

3. What does "borrowing" the faith of someone else mean to you? How do you think it can be done?

ACTION ITEMS

Pick out two or three areas in which you find it difficult to have faith and write them down. Now, start praying daily for God to increase your faith in these areas and decide how to act on those prayers to do what you can to make it happen.

CHAPTER TWENTY-SEVEN

Live By Faith!

—Theresa Ferguson

"We live by faith, not by sight." (2 Corinthians 5:7)

Paul could confidently say these words because his life was characterized by faith in God to work in all circumstances. We, as Christians today, strive to imitate the faith seen in the life of Paul and of Christ himself. Our faith in God to work out everything for his purposes is demonstrated in the following areas.

Faith in Unity

As disciples of Jesus, we are unified with a common purpose to love God (Matthew 37-40), to win as many as possible (1 Corinthians 9:19-23), and to present each person perfect in Christ (Colossians 1: 28). In these three areas, we must truly have a trusting faith to believe that God is working in each of our lives. Staying focused on being used in these areas is a matter of consistent motivation, and we must help each other gain and maintain this focus. What a blessing to be unified in faith with our brothers and sisters!

We can be effective for God when each part of the family is working together as one (Ephesians 4:16). The principle of synergism can be seen plainly in physical examples. Once in Canada during a weight pulling contest, the best two horses pulled about 9,000 pounds apiece. Yoked together, however, they pulled nearly 30,000 pounds! Unity works, and synergism is best seen in the sharing of spiritual purposes. People can achieve more working together than whatever their individual efforts could ever accomplish.

Faith in Changes

We can see the results of living by faith when we see the necessity for change. Our initial human tendency is to avoid changes and even dread them. But there can be no growth without change. When we embrace changes and respond willingly and humbly to them, our faith grows. When reorganizations in churches are necessary, this means new leaders and new brothers and sisters in our groups. By faith, these changes should cause us to excitedly anticipate new opportunities to grow in faith. These new opportunities also expose areas in our character that God can and will change.

It is true that change can produce fear in us, but in looking back at various stages of our lives, wouldn't you agree that most of those fears turned out to be irrational? Instead of expecting the worst outcomes, what if we expect the best? One principle must be kept in mind, the same one weightlifters put in these common words: no pain, no gain! God is always working to help us build our faith muscles, but how does he most often accomplish this goal? Is it not through the testing of our faith? It would be nice if faith grew easily and effortlessly, but we know that is not the case. Our greatest growth comes when we have faced and overcome challenges – the challenges of change. What a joy to have our faith tested by change!

Faith in Fruitfulness

It is a great privilege to be a copartner with the God of the universe in producing fruit. One of the most exciting and rewarding experiences possible is leading another person to Christ. To teach someone how to be transformed from darkness to light is to participate in a miracle! We need to walk by faith in believing that God will make us fruitful, leading us to open people and open people to us. No matter how ineffective you may feel, you really can lead someone else to Christ. Just work toward that end as you pray and trust God for the results. Remember that this process begins by opening your mouth to start building a relationship. Prayerfully, when you share about the great things God has done in your life, your new friends will respond favorably. Personal testimonies often have an amazing impact and naturally lead into a shared open Bible.

Putting two verses together can help build our faith in this vital area. 1 Timothy 2:4 assures us that God "wants all people to be saved and to come to a knowledge of the truth." Then in John 5:17, Jesus made this statement: "My Father is always at his work to this very day, and I too am working." When you look at these verses together, you know that God wants everyone to become his child and that he is always working to see Christians and non-Christians meet for that purpose. Trust him in that and keep your eyes, ears and mouth open to discover who he is causing your paths to cross. You have heard stories of the most unusual circumstances leading two people together to bring one of them to salvation. Let God create such a story for you. To that end he is working, so let's join him and be used to bear the fruit of salvation!

Faith in Developing Maturity

After the miracle of rebirth comes the exciting experience of maturing as a Christian. Our faith in God can grow each day as we see ourselves and others overcoming problems. Even when the solutions are not obvious, he can lead us to victory if we will keep trusting him. Philippians 4:13 is often quoted in this context and for good reason: "We can do all things through Christ who gives us strength!"

Not only can we develop maturity by overcoming problems, but we can also develop additional skills. Rest assured that our new leaders in various capacities will be much more capable this time next year. As we do our part, God will more than do his. Even when we cannot see where all the future leaders will come from, God already knows and is raising them up even now. He wants to mature all of us and will put us in positions where he can work through us. We may not see ourselves as leaders, but God can use us to lead others by our examples and by our efforts to keep growing. One of the greatest motivators is in watching another person grow into maturity out of areas in which they were formerly immature. Just trust him and live each day by faith!

QUESTIONS FOR THOUGHT

1. How unified do you feel with the fellow disciples in your present ministry? Who could you start reaching out to and build greater unity of purpose together?

2. What kind of changes do you anticipate positively and what kind do you anticipate negatively? How can you change those negative feelings?

3. Rate your level of faith in leading others to Christ and rate your level of faith in changing things about yourself that need changing.

ACTION ITEMS

This chapter discussed faith in four areas: unity, change, fruitfulness, and maturity. Choose something from each of these four areas and do one thing in each this week to build your faith. Every journey starts with the first step and that includes the journey toward deeper faith in action.

CHAPTER TWENTY-EIGHT

Be Strong in the Grace

—Gordon Ferguson

"You then, my son, be strong in the grace that is in Christ Jesus." (2 Timothy 2:1)

When you hear the word, *grace,* what comes first to your mind? Perhaps you think "unmerited favor" or a similar definition. Or maybe you come up with: "forgiveness which we do not deserve yet still receive." The concept of grace is multifaceted, so we will focus on six aspects of grace reflected in a passage written by the apostle Paul. Applying each of them in our lives is vitally important.

2 Timothy 2:1-8

¹ You then, my son, be strong in the grace that is in Christ Jesus. ² And the things you have heard me say in the presence of many witnesses entrust to reliable people who will also be qualified to teach others. ³ Join with me in suffering, like a good soldier of Christ Jesus. ⁴ No one serving as a soldier gets entangled in civilian affairs, but rather tries to please his commanding officer. ⁵ Similarly, anyone who competes as an athlete does not receive the victor's crown except by competing according to the rules. ⁶ The hardworking farmer should be the first to receive a share of the crops. ⁷ Reflect on what I am saying, for the Lord will give you insight into all this. ⁸ Remember Jesus Christ, raised from the dead, descended from David. This is my gospel...

Initially, we must understand that grace not only embodies forgiveness; it can strengthen us as well. If we don't move from the former to the latter, life is going to beat us down and beat us up. Simply focusing on being forgiven may also keep us focused on our sins, whereas seeing grace as giving us the strength to resist sin provides encouragement and confidence. So how can we be strong in the grace that is in Christ Jesus? This passage not only gives us the answer to that question but if we have ears to hear, we can be awakened to our desperate need for the strength grace provides.

First, be strong in sharing your faith (verse 2). I have heard people ask why the New Testament doesn't emphasize sharing our faith as much as our family of churches historically has. It's a good question, isn't it? While we have to admit that some of the motivation used to promote evangelism was faulty, reaching out to others with the gospel is surely a part of following Jesus. For starters, we do have the Great Commission, right (Matthew 28:18-20)? We do have the example of Jesus and his mission to seek and save the lost (Luke 19:10). We do have the example of the early church and its amazing growth. The driving principle supporting the importance of sharing our faith is found in Acts 4:20 – "As for us, we cannot help speaking about what we have seen and heard." Sharing our faith is giving our testimony, which Revelation 12:11 tells us is a part of overcoming Satan. It will definitely increase our faith.

Second, be strong as a suffering soldier of Christ (verses 3-4). Paul mentions suffering and refusing to get "entangled in civilian affairs." Life is challenging and suffering is inevitable. Enduring suffering will either prove to be a stumbling block or a stepping-stone, but we cannot mature spiritually without hard times. Learn to embrace them. Unfortunately, some of us get wimpy with lots of grumbling and complaining. The civilian affairs which we are to avoid becoming entangled in could be ordinary affairs or culturally driven affairs. I believe good examples of ordinary affairs are mentioned in the Parable of the Sower as "the worries of the world, the deceitfulness of riches, and the desires for other things (Mark 4:19)." Once these take root, the vibrancy of the Word is choked out and it becomes unfruitful in our lives. I believe the way people act (and post on social media) about politics is a prime example of a culturally driven affair. It seems like some folks believe their favored political party holds the answers for all our problems. If it's not politics, there are plenty of other "causes" (like WOKE gone crazy!) that people get entangled in that causes them to miss the strength available in the grace of Jesus. Staying focused on being a soldier of Christ will keep us focused on his cause and will strengthen us in his grace.

Third, be strong as a rule-following athlete (verse 5). I am reminded of the writer of Hebrews who encourages us to run the "race set before us" with perseverance by "fixing our eyes on Jesus" (Hebrews 12:1-3). This race of life is decidedly a marathon, not a 100-meter sprint. Old age ain't for sissies, says the tee shirt, and staying in the race doesn't become easier as you get older. Paul also says that we must run according to the rules. Less and less people in our society even know what God's biblical rules are. Any of us can start watering down the rules to avoid the commitment involved in a life fully devoted to God. My fears when the pandemic struck was that we would become too comfortable sitting in our pajamas watching virtual church services, and that fear was not unfounded. Zoom has its place, but being a part of an actual fellowship service will always be needed. Christianity by design is a "one another," "each other" relationship focused religion. Relationships with others help keep our commitment level high.

Fourth, be strong as a hardworking farmer (verse 6). Farming is a hard job. In my youth, I spent many days on the farms of relatives. Those days started at about 4:30 a.m. and were filled with chores that left me bone tired by the end of the day. But God designed us to work—chilling can be killing! Idleness is indeed the devil's workshop. Even in our 80s, both Theresa and I strive to make every day count by having some type of impact on others spiritually. I suppose at 82 years of age, you could say I am retired, but I have been writing this material most of the day. Since writing is one of my spiritual gifts, I intend to use it until it becomes impossible. Sitting around watching TV all day or reading novels or playing golf or any one of many other ways to pass time is never going to be my "gig." Maybe I am a workaholic (probably am) but I don't feel any guilt reading this verse, that's for sure! Staying engaged keeps us growing at any age.

Fifth, be strong in seeking Christ's insights (verse 7). God gives insights to those who seek them. As I mentioned in the chapter about not being a foster child to God, I pray daily for the Holy Spirit (Luke 11:13), who definitely gives insights. I love Philippians 3:15-16, which promises that God will continue to give us insights if we are putting into practice what we already understand. If we really want answers to our challenges, we can find them with the help of the Holy Spirit. But as always, hindsight will trump foresight most of the time! We must stay busy and obedient if God is going to reveal those insights which will lead us even higher, increasing our spiritual strength through his grace.

Sixth, be strong in keeping Christ as your focus (verse 8). It is most fitting that the passage finishes on this point, for it is the most important of all. If "all the treasures of wisdom and knowledge" are hidden in Christ (Colossians 2:3), then keeping our focus on him must be paramount. I recall preaching a sermon a few years back entitled, "Is Your Religion Focused on Christ or the Church?" Whatever you focus on is what you will see most prominently; and unless your gaze is fixed on Jesus, you will be tempted to be hyper critical of whatever else is in your sights. The church is made up of humans, and if you focus on all the imperfections that are easily visible, you soon will see mostly that. This principle is true when applied to any human or human institution, certainly including the church.

I often say that I am the biggest critic remaining in our family of churches, but I am a critic speaking up and trying to help—not an armchair quarterback. Do we have flaws and dysfunction in the church? Of course, for it is comprised of fallible humans like you and me. As my friend, John Louis, often says: "dysfunction is the gift that keeps on giving." If we can handle dysfunction in our physical families and keep on loving, how can we do less in our spiritual family? My focus is on Jesus, with whom my days begin and end. That keeps all else in perspective and keeps me in the spiritual battle as a soldier, an athlete and a hardworking farmer. In other words, it keeps me strong in the grace!

QUESTIONS FOR THOUGHT

1. How would you now define and describe grace differently after reading this chapter?

2. How does the thought of being a spiritual soldier register on you? A rule-keeping athlete? A hardworking farmer? Which offers you the biggest challenge to contemplate?

3. Could you honestly say that Jesus is your highest focus in life? Explain it to yourself.

ACTION ITEMS

In which ways are you strongest in grace and in which are you weakest? In a journal, rank them in order, then write down some steps to help you make the strong ones stronger and the weak ones stronger as well. Share your findings with a spiritual friend as you commit to act on your steps to strengthen your grace walk.

CHAPTER TWENTY-NINE

Content, but Not Complacent

—Theresa Ferguson

"I have learned the secret of being content in any and every situation.." (Philippians 4:12)

Jesus had a heart to meet the needs of people. He emptied himself to give us all we need (Philippians 2:7). He became poor to make us rich (2 Corinthians 8:9), and by this, he taught us the meaning of life as we follow and imitate him. I want to address hospitality with this definition in mind: a giving of yourself to others.

In response to someone who wanted to follow him Jesus said, "Foxes have holes and birds of the air have nests, but the Son of Man has no place to lay his head (Matthew 8:20)." Yet, Jesus was content with what he had; he was not dependent on material possessions. Without possessions (much less nice ones), he was able to influence people and change the world!

Give What You Have

Neither the security nor the happiness of our Lord was tied to physical things. He could have possessed anything he desired, but his contentment had absolutely nothing to do with the physical. He was unimpressed with and unencumbered by *things*. Therefore, he never let his showing of hospitality be hindered by what he had or didn't have materially. We learn from Jesus that hospitality has everything to do with meeting the needs of people, and little to do with the quality of the setting where it is practiced, or the quantity of goods consumed. His focus was on fellowship and love.

Did Jesus think it was wrong to have houses and possessions? We know the answer to that question is "No" as we see him reclining at the house of his friends in Bethany (John 12:2). God had blessed them with worldly wealth, and they were faithful stewards of what they had been given. They used their blessings to serve others. The point that Jesus made with his spartan lifestyle was that contentment does not come because of anything we have or do not have.

The apostle Paul later modeled his contentment after Jesus, although he informs us it was something he *learned:*

Philippians 4:11-13

[11] I am not saying this because I am in need, for I have learned to be content whatever the circumstances. [12] I know what it is to be in need, and I know what it is to have plenty. I have learned the secret of being content in any and every situation, whether well fed or hungry, whether living in plenty or in want. [13] I can do everything through him who gives me strength.

Further, he challenged us to follow his example of contentment by trusting that "God will meet all your needs according to his glorious riches in Christ Jesus" (Philippians 4:19). When we allow God to meet our spiritual and emotional needs, we can have the proper perspective regarding our physical needs.

Contentment is a prerequisite of effective hospitality. We often see our physical circumstances as vital to the practice of hospitality and can allow discontentment with those things to hinder us from being hospitable. Nothing could be less like Jesus and his early leaders. They were concerned with loving people, not impressing them. Our clear call is to do the same, with or without nice possessions or living quarters. Contentment with our lives means being content with our marriages, children, salary, geographic location, and especially with the house or apartment God has provided! Let's give up our love of the world (see 1 John 2:15), be content with our physical settings, and share what we have with open and humble hearts as Jesus did.

A Challenge to My Character!

Through the years, moving has provided the biggest challenge to my contentment level. Since Gordon and I married 60 years ago, we have lived in over 30 different houses or apartments. As we have gotten older, our moving from one residence to another has not slowed down. We lived in Boston longer than anywhere during our marriage (16 years), and there we lived in 9 different places. Obviously, God has been working on my character to bring me to a deeper understanding of contentment!

At our wedding, a soloist sang a song based on the book of Ruth containing these words: "Whither thou goest, I will go; whither thou lodgest, I will lodge." After having "lodged" in one house for my first 18 years, I could not have imagined what the words of that song would mean in my married life! Had I been able to foresee the future at that time from my humble Louisiana roots, I would have fainted!

As a non-Christian, possessions were very important in my search for the "great American Dream." By my mid-20s, Gordon and I had been successful in our pursuit of possessions. We bought a house, sold it, and proceeded to buy an even bigger one. We also acquired new furniture, cars, a fishing camp with lake frontage and a private pier, five acres of land on which to build our dream house, and numerous other items. During these early years, we saw each move as a step up the ladder of success. Although possessions seemed to provide security and contentment, the good feelings were short-lived. Soon the newness wore off, and the feelings of emptiness returned.

The empty feelings were no doubt a big part of our motivation to seek lasting fulfillment in spiritual things. In our late 20s, we caught the dream of serving God full-time. We sold nearly all our possessions and moved to another state for Gordon to attend a ministry training school. Our nice, suburban home was exchanged for a dumpy apartment in a dangerous area, but we were happier and more content than we had ever been. It became clear just how little physical possessions figured into true happiness.

I was six months pregnant with our second child when Gordon completed his initial two years of training. We then moved 2,000 miles from our parents and other close family members. To add to the challenge, my favorite aunt (who was more like my grandmother) was dying of cancer. Now feelings of guilt and grief added to my burdens and made for a rough transition. In all of this, God was calling for me to be content. However, I had not yet learned the lesson. Instead, I learned to "stuff" my feelings and act contented, while deep inside, I felt sorry for myself and for my children. God had much more work to do on my character!

In our numerous ministry moves, my focus was on the struggles of Gordon and the children and on helping them to be content. Although I poured myself into my work as a minister's wife and mother of two, contentment remained an elusive reality. My character did not ultimately change until I became a true disciple of Jesus just before moving to Boston. I had been religious, but I did not have the indwelling power of the Holy Spirit to transform my heart. I finally learned to put Philippians 4 into practice in dealing with my emotions. Praise God for these victories and for the deep sense of contentment present in my life now on a daily basis!

Contentment in Action

When we are not content, practicing hospitality is forced and unnatural. However, when we are content, hospitality is a natural expression of our gratitude. We want to share when we have something to share. We get excited about spreading love through hospitality, and our creative juices begin to flow. Crimped budgets and cramped living quarters will matter little when our hearts are full of love, joy and peace.

As we talk of being content in all circumstances, we must be careful not to confuse contentment with complacency. We must not reason, "My surroundings don't matter. I must be content with these dark curtains that make my house seem depressing to everyone who enters." We can be resourceful and use what we have to brighten our homes and make them welcoming, no matter how humble. But we must not find our security in the amount or the quality of the things we own.

Once we begin to imitate Jesus in meeting the needs of as many as possible, our relationships will blossom, and we will have joyous memories of serving others. Some of my best memories are when others lived with us during times of special need in their lives. We denied ourselves more than normal, sometimes giving up our bedroom for months at a time. The inconveniences proved to be minor, but the rewards were great. We can never out-give God; and giving through hospitality is one of the best ways to discover this truth. Let's decide to be truly content and show hospitality like never before. It is a demonstration of the heart of God!

QUESTIONS FOR THOUGHT

1. On a scale of 1-10, how content are you with your material possessions? Explain your answer.

2. Think of the most content person in their life setting that you know. What do you think makes them so content?

3. What are the conditions that make it easy for you to practice hospitality? What makes it hard for you to show hospitality? In what ways can you grow to become a more hospitable person?

ACTION ITEMS

Have a talk with your spouse if you are married, or your closest friends if you are not, and examine your present level of showing hospitality. Make specific plans to grow in this area.

CHAPTER THIRTY

Caged Up or Cut Out?

—Theresa Ferguson

"For the word of God is alive and active. Sharper than any double-edged sword, it penetrates even to dividing soul and spirit, joints and marrow; it judges the thoughts and attitudes of the heart. Nothing in all creation is hidden from God's sight. Everything is uncovered and laid bare before the eyes of him to whom we must give account." (Hebrews 4:12-13)

As women, we cringe at the thought of being caged up by someone or something. We also have a fear of something being cut out of us! However, we must make a choice between the two: either we will be caged up by Satan because of our sins, or we will let God cut the sins out of our lives.

Caged Up by Satan

In Hebrews 4, the Israelites were used as an example of those who remained caged up because of a lack of faith in God and an unwillingness to repent. Their disobedience prohibited them from entering the rest in the promised land that God was willing to provide. Similarly, we cage ourselves up by our own sins. The only solution is to allow God and his word to cut the sin out of our lives, penetrating down even to our thoughts and motives as the scripture above relates. He is the Great Physician and the Master Heart Surgeon.

A close friend once used a memorable example illustrating how we can remain caged up because of a lack of faith in God. The story was about a brown bear purchased by a zoo in Heidelberg, Germany, from a traveling circus. While owned by the circus, the bear had spent his entire life cooped up in a cage only 12 feet long. He paced back and forth in the cage every waking hour in conditions that were described as terrible, at best. He was ill-fed and ill-treated but lived to continue his frantic march—12 feet forward and 12 feet back. The new owners of the zoo assumed that the bear would be delighted with his spacious new compound. But alas, such was not the case. The bear ignored the open door to his cage until he was driven from the cage by the attendants. Once inside his new spacious surroundings, he immediately began to pace the exact same dimensions of his former cage. When the bear could not be released from the cage in his mind, the zoo officials finally decided to end his misery by euthanizing him.

The application is rather obvious. We can be caged up by Satan and our own sins and not even be aware of it. Even with the promise of freedom provided by God, we continue to live life in the same sinful patterns that we learned from youth. This is a scary thought to me! How did you feel when you read the story of the bear? Did it make you search your heart and mind to see what sins Satan has been using to keep you captive? It should have! The bear did not have a choice about being caged up for most of his life—but we do. God can do miracles in bringing about life changes in us, and whether those changes come quickly or slowly, by God's power they will come.

Cut Out by God

According to Hebrews 4, when we are encaged and experiencing a lack of faith in God and his power to set us free, we begin entertaining sinful thoughts that lead to sinful behaviors. In my life, I have been caged up by entertaining negative thoughts about myself, by fearing people, by harboring resentments, and by being controlled by self-pity, sentimentality and insecurity! I hate these sins that held me captive for so long, especially when I see how they affected the lives of my family. Without realizing it, I was teaching my loved ones the same pattern of life I was living!

God hates the sins in our lives to the point of being angry about them (Hebrews 4:3), because he knows that they will ultimately harden our hearts (Hebrews 4:7). We need to be nauseated about being enslaved by our sins; and we should run to God to be cut loose from them. Are you willing to let him cut out your sins? It will take four things on our part to be completely set free:

1. We must make the decision to do it! We must give God the opportunity to lay open the true condition of our souls (all the good and the bad). As women, we don't like pain, but there is no gain without it! Otherwise, we go through life being deceived into thinking we are right with God when we are still locked up in the cage of sin.

2. Discipleship is God's finest tool in doing corrective surgery on our hearts. Are you eager to be corrected, taught and confronted about the sins in your life? God's word is powerful, but it will not do the job until it is seriously applied to our lives. And it cannot be applied by us alone—others usually see us more clearly than we see ourselves. We must give them the opportunity to help us experience freedom by providing us with a good mixture of correction and encouragement.

3. The most effective demonstration of how to defeat Satan is best seen in the life of Jesus. He defeated Satan at every turn, and now helps us do the same. "Let us then approach God's throne of grace with confidence, so that we may receive mercy and find grace to help us in our time of need" (Hebrews 4:16). This confidence comes from what the previous verse in Hebrews 4 says, "For we do not have a high priest who is unable to empathize with our weaknesses, but we have one who has been tempted in every way, just as we are—yet he did not sin."

4. We must not depend on our own strength and ability. We were not meant to carry the heavy burdens of life alone. Jesus has promised that he will make our burden light: "Take my yoke upon you and learn from me, for I am gentle and humble in heart, and you will find rest for your souls. For my yoke is easy and my burden is light" (Matthew 11:29-30).

As God's indestructible women, we must be willing and eager to be changed by him to be freed from Satan's cage. It is our choice: will we be caged up by Satan or cut out by God?

QUESTIONS FOR THOUGHT

1. What sins are keeping you caged and killing your joy? Pray as you list them.

2. What sinful patterns have you seen regularly crop up in your life? Remember that patterns have a starting point and foundation. What's yours?

3. Are you sharing with your close friends the sins that are enslaving you?

ACTION ITEMS

Invite your circle of close Christian friends over and help each other identify patterns of sin that are keeping you enslaved and ineffective in your Christian walk.

CHAPTER THIRTY-ONE

Overcoming Fears

—Theresa Ferguson

"For the Spirit God gave us does not make us timid, but gives us power, love and self-discipline. So do not be ashamed of the testimony about our Lord or of me his prisoner. Rather, join me in suffering for the gospel, by the power of God." (2 Timothy 1:7-8)

For much of my life I have struggled with a paralyzing fear and distrust of people. When we moved from San Diego to Boston, Massachusetts in early 1988 and placed membership with a church there, it became evident that I did not really trust even my closest relationships. I did not trust my husband, my children, or even God in heaven. My lack of trust and fear of being emotionally hurt by others had caused me to put up a wall around my emotions. This defense of fear and distrust prevented others from being able to hurt me, but it also stopped them from being able to help me.

Thank God for discipling! He used Wyndham and Jeanie Shaw, along with Gordon, to love me enough to delve into my life and help me overcome some of my biggest fears of people. I want to share some of my personal struggles with fear and mistrust and offer some practical suggestions that I have used and am using to be victorious over the main culprit: fear.

My Backstory of Causes and Its Evidence

The causes of my mistrust began with having an alcoholic father whose frequent violent actions and rejection caused me to mistrust men in general. Through the years, I became increasingly mistrustful of even religious men due to bad experiences with leaders in the church I attended. Additionally, my husband, who was a minister, was sometimes harsh and insensitive toward my feelings.

The evidence of my mistrust was exhibited in my reluctance to voice my opinions in discussions with leaders. I was so focused on what their response to my words might be that I just retreated into silence. My lack of interest in developing friendships with any person in authority or any man with a dominant personality was another demonstration of mistrust. Further, I responded to new challenges as a Christian with an "Oh, no!" followed by "but I will do it." I also retreated from any type of confrontational or controversial discussions with close friends and even with my husband.

In overcoming a lack of trust, five items have been especially helpful to me. **First,** I decided to be truthful about my deepest feelings. I began expressing all my feelings and then allowed others to show me which feelings might be based on faulty or irrational thinking. I made the decision to spill it all out on the table like a puzzle and then allow others to help me sort out the lies and truths of my emotional makeup. I decided to quit believing the lies from Satan and to crucify any sinful attitudes that were contributing to my fears. I was reminded of the words of the Apostle John: "There is no fear in love. But perfect love drives out fear, because fear has to do with punishment. The one who fears is not made perfect in love" (1 John 4:18).

The most difficult aspect of openness was deciding to let down my emotional protection. I started this process with Gordon, Wyndham, and Jeanie, only after they assured me that they would be trustworthy with my words and emotions. At first it was difficult (and even scary) to be so vulnerable with genuine transparency, but it resulted in the wonderful healing promised by God in James 5:16: "Therefore confess your sins to each other and pray for each other so that you may be healed. The prayer of a righteous person is powerful and effective."

Second, I decided to reveal all my resentments and hurts. I wrote out a list of all my hurts, how I reacted to them, and then the sins I committed in response to the hurts. When I saw that my sins were just as bad as the hurts themselves, I was able to quickly forgive those who had hurt me. Now, I'm free, forgiven and released to be all that God wants me to be.

Third, I had to understand and accept that God was a perfect Parent. A book that a friend had given to Gordon entitled, *Trusting God Even When Life Hurts,* helped me to emotionally accept God as the ideal Father that I did not have as a child. God gave me everything that I needed to be transformed through suffering into the likeness of Christ. The hard times I experienced were now being used by God to help me develop a strong character that would be an example for others (Romans 5:3-5).

Fourth, I started to earnestly seek discipling. (As the Bible teaches it, not as some have wrongly practiced it.) Discipleship is truly God's perfect plan to help all of us grow continually in trust and confidence. We must seek discipling from whomever he puts into our lives and accept all of life's experiences as a part of the process. All things do work together for good if we keep loving, trusting, and obeying him (Romans 8:28).

Fifth, I had to consciously transfer the focus off myself and onto God and others. I began my daily worship time by reading scriptures that addressed the area of trust. Books like Psalms and Isaiah were most helpful. I consistently pray for more trust in my relationships and experiences. Concerning my treatment of others, I focus on these qualities of love described in 1 Corinthians 13:

1 Corinthians 13:4-7

"Love is patient, love is kind. It does not envy, it does not boast, it is not proud. It does not dishonor others, it is not self-seeking, it is not easily angered, it keeps no record of wrongs. Love does not delight in evil but rejoices with the truth. It always protects, always trusts, always hopes, always perseveres"

In conclusion, these five items: truthfulness, revealing resentments, understanding that God is a perfect parent, seeking discipling, and transferring focus off myself—do more than spell **TRUST**; they absolutely develop and sustain it. Today, I am a happy woman in God's kingdom because I have committed to trust him even when life hurts! I pray that you will make that same kind of decision!

QUESTIONS FOR THOUGHT

1. What events in your life have most contributed to your fears?

2. How have fears kept you from growing in your faith?

3. What does it mean that "perfect love casts out fear" (1 John 4:18)?

ACTION ITEMS

Contact at least two of your closest friends and begin sharing your greatest fears. Shine light on your darkest fears and do not let them imprison you.

CHAPTER THIRTY-TWO

Learning to Forgive and Helping Others Learn to Forgive, Part 1

—Theresa Ferguson

"For if you forgive men when they sin against you, your heavenly Father will also forgive you. But if you do not forgive men their sins, your Father will not forgive your sins." (Matthew 6:14-15)

Did you read that passage carefully? If you do not forgive people, God will treat you the same way. Yet, this command is designed to bless us. Being unforgiving, resentful, and bitter destroys our own hearts, while forgiveness is the path to a peaceful heart. God has helped me to learn how to forgive, and I want to help others learn to forgive. God is quite serious about this subject. It is not an optional matter.

The Need

Every day we face the question "Will I forgive?" All family members hurt one another. Church family members also hurt each other. Especially challenging is forgiving church leaders who have hurt us. We will never outgrow our need to forgive every day, just as we ask God to forgive us of our sins.

How can you tell when someone needs forgiveness at a deeper level? If anyone stays consistently weak, something inside them is likely unresolved. If fears and mistrust are evident in one's demeanor and actions, forgiveness is almost certainly lacking. Even if we learn to hide signs of unforgiveness, we still need to expose and deal with them. Often, our unresolved emotional issues have to do with relational conflicts or abuse in our early years. By learning how to forgive as we face our own past, we can be an instrument of God to free up others through helping them learn to forgive. I am eager to share this material with you because it has helped so many learn to forgive. I want you to learn to go through the process that I am going to describe.

Finding Out the Facts

It is very important to describe God's plan for forgiving those who have hurt us. I began to use this process when I was working things out in my own life. My father was an alcoholic, and in working through the hurt I had in my relationship with him, God has transformed my heart toward my father, men in general and my husband. When you become a disciple after many years of marriage, like I did, you probably have a lot of baggage to work through.

I had really shut down emotionally, which is what most of us with alcoholic parents do for protection from the pain. My father was a great father when I was in my early childhood years, but as I got older, he became very abusive. In the last couple of years that I lived at home, it was like hell on earth. In looking back, I realized that just a couple of instances hurt me the most. When I thought of my father, I just wanted to cry, and I never seemed to have enough tears to get it all cried out. However, because of being able to work through my pain, I have learned how to help other people work through theirs. In the following material, I am going to focus on how to help others with their need to forgive, but the same principles will help you deal with your own need to forgive.

Begin by asking questions of yourself and others and listening for what is in the heart. For instance, if a person has lost their love for other people and has bitterness in their heart against someone, ask, "When did this begin?" Listen and listen and listen some more. Let them totally get out what they are feeling. Then find out if they have an abusive background: sexually, physically, or emotionally. (One is not necessarily more damaging than the others.) Talk with them about how they are doing spiritually. Ask, "What were you like when you were first baptized? Tell me about your love for other people. Tell me about your faith." And then

ask, "What happened to it?" Many times, it boils down to a relationship problem with a leader or with another brother or sister in
Christ. Then continue to ask more questions. Maybe they are mad
at God—many people blame God for difficult times in their lives
and become bitter toward him.

Proceed by probing deeper into their early years: "Tell me just a
little bit about your family. What was the relationship like between
your parents? Are they still married? What was your relationship
like in the early years with your father? What were the good things
in your relationship with him? What were the hurtful things in your
relationship with him?" Then go through the same questions about
their mom and their siblings. From asking questions like these, you
will discover a lot of hurt in most everyone's background. Some
will have worked through these things already, but many will need
help in facing and overcoming the emotional damage.

When we first become disciples, we repent of all our sins, and
we feel like we can do anything and everything! And we can. But
the longer we are disciples, the more our past hurts may re-sur-
face, affecting our love and faith levels. If this happens, we must
deal with it or lose our spiritual drive and become bitter. On our
decade birthdays (thirty, forty, fifty especially), we often think,
"How do I feel about my life? How do I feel about my past?" As
we get older in the Lord and older chronologically, we often have
more things that come up from our past. When this happens, we
must come to terms with it if we are to be at peace emotionally.

TIME TO BEGIN WRITING

Facing the Truth

Once the details of a person's past have been talked out and
the main source of hurts discovered, it is time for them to begin
writing. In one column, have them write down, "Facing the
Truth." As they write under this heading, they must face the reality
of what happened to them. "What are the things that someone
said or did that hurt you?" Painful memories signal that we have
unfinished business, for we are not yet free from the hold these

experiences have on us. Have them write John 8:31-32 at the top of that column, because they must face the truth about the situation. Whoever they have a problem with, have them write down what was specifically said or done that hurt them.

Many of us can have flashbacks that we don't understand. We do not know where they come from, and we are afraid of them. Explain the following:

> "Such thoughts are like a puzzle that you need help figuring out and putting together. As you write down what someone said or did to hurt you, we are going to put this puzzle together. Then you will be able to see the big picture and understand it. The painful memories should be viewed simply like a visitor from your past who is coming to talk to you and tell you something that will help you. And God is going to help you face the past and gain the victory."

At this point, I will generally read a passage such as Psalm 18 to help them see that God is on their side and point out the comforting lessons as we read verse by verse.

Feeling the Hurts

In the second column, have them write "Feeling the Hurts." They have to feel the pain once more, which often will be as the pain of a child if their traumatic experience occurred in childhood. Just say,

"I want you to write down what happened when you were hurt, even if you can only remember a certain portion of it. Then I want you to write that person a letter—which you will not mail—to really get in touch with the pain of those experiences. When you write the person a letter, express it as you felt when the hurts occurred."

> We can want to deny the pain in our past, and say, "Oh, it's going to be okay. That shouldn't have happened anyway." It can be very difficult to face our unresolved pain, but bad things happen when we do not deal with it:

anger turns to resentment, which turns to bitterness, and finally, apathy. But God is not pleased with apathy, for we simply quit feeling for the person who hurt us.

The person you are helping may say, "I don't know if I have apathy." Say to them, "What if the person came into the room right now, would you initiate with them? Would you go greet them? Would you share the gospel with them?" If you are reluctant to share God's Word with someone, then you do not really love them. Even when we hate their sin, we must still love their soul, just like God does with us.

If a person is afraid to write these negative feelings out alone, for fear that they may be overcome with rage, let them do it in your house while you are present—even if you are doing other chores. They will have to deal with these emotions to escape the grasp of Satan. When they get everything out into the light, his power is greatly diminished. Maybe they are not angry toward someone who hurt them personally, but their anger is felt toward someone who hurt someone else they were close to.

Their greatest emotion may be fear. Our fears will either cause us to deny reality or to run from it by shutting down. We may shut down on the outside while screaming on the inside. The point is that we must get in touch with the emotions produced by what we experienced if we want to get well.

As someone writes this letter, they are encountering all the different feelings they have about the experience—shame or even guilt for having the negative emotions at all. They cannot allow themself to rationalize away what happened; it must be dealt with adequately. After someone writes the letter, usually I have them come and read it to me. It is amazing what happens to people when they do get the gunk out in the light of day. They usually feel, "Hey, I have just become a whole person from reading this because now I'm on the outside reading about this and it's not controlling me." And very often, their emotions will change even from writing the letter.

QUESTIONS FOR THOUGHT

1. As you read this, what were the strongest thoughts and feelings that came to your mind and emotions?

2. How do you feel about digging into the hurts in your own past? Are you willing to do it to please God and find peace?

3. If you sense that you have unfinished business in forgiving others, will you ask a trusted friend to help you walk through this process?

ACTION ITEMS

Pray for two things. One, for yourself, that you will see your own need to forgive and who it is that you need to forgive. Two, for others that you believe carry unresolved relationship hurts in their heart. Then after reading Part 2, write out your plans to get help and give help.

CHAPTER THIRTY-THREE

Learning to Forgive and Helping Others Learn to Forgive, Part 2

—Theresa Ferguson

"For if you forgive men when they sin against you, your heavenly Father will also forgive you. But if you do not forgive men their sins, your Father will not forgive your sins." (Matthew 6:14-15)

Facing Your Sins

In the third column, write, "Facing Your Sins." No matter what may have been done to someone, they have almost certainly sinned in response in some way (most often with anger and bitterness). A part of their healing must be repentance from sinful responses and from keeping a record of wrongs. No two people respond the same way when sins are committed against them, even when they are in the same family. One person will forgive and not even remember the incident, while the other person can become so bitter against the one who hurt them that they hold on to an incident for the rest of their life. It is easy to rationalize our bitterness, leading to confessing without real conviction. Do not underestimate the power of truly repenting of your own sins, even if they seem minor compared to the sins committed against you.

At this point I always use the example of Jesus. His heart was freed from holding resentments against people. On the cross he said, "Forgive them for they know not what they do." We must forgive those who sin against us and surrender them and the outcomes to God.

An Issue of Trust

Under the third column on "Facing Your Sins," have the person write the word "TRUST." Each letter of the word will stand for another word that will help them in the forgiveness process. Share the following with the person (the parts in quotation marks):

T – *take responsibility* for your own sin. For example, "If you were sexually abused, your sin was not that you let the person abuse you (though some tend to mistakenly blame themselves). Your sin is that you have been bitter toward the perpetrator all these years. You must own up to your sins and confess them specifically (James 5:16)."

R – *respond in prayer.* "Surrender the anger, the fear, the bitterness, or any other sin. As a disciple, your response in prayer leaves you not only forgiven, but healed (James 5:16). Now, let's you and I pray right now that you can give up that anger. In a few minutes, I'm going to ask you to surrender it and really give it up for the last time." (Then pray together about it and do it.)

U – *understand that God will judge* and punish the person who sinned against you, and that God loves that person more than you do. "According to Romans 12:17-21, God will hold this person responsible for all the things that were done and said that hurt you. Even if a person seems to get off in this life, the scales will be balanced in eternity if they do not repent. Plus, God has given them consequences right now in trying to help them wake up."

S – *surrender it all emotionally to God.* "You need to change your mind about holding on to the list in the first column. You have written it all out, talked it all out and expressed every bit of it. You have changed your mind, and you want to let go and let God. Now pray about it and give it up: 'God, help me surrender this to you. Forgive me for keeping a record of these wrongs. Forgive [the person] for hurting me.' Not that the person gets forgiven at that point by God, but your heart is merciful. Emotionally, you are making a break from the bonds that have held you back." (Then end the surrender process by either tearing up or burning up the letter—our gas grill has often been used for this step.)

T — *thankful to God for the victory.* "Looking back to Romans 12:9, the opening admonition is that our 'love must be sincere.' You know, brother or sister, God loves you so sincerely. He's forgiven you, and he's so happy that you have the heart now to forgive and that you have forgiven [name the person]. You know the sincere love I have for you because I've helped you work through this. Most importantly, you know the sincere love that Jesus had for you, because in the Garden of Gethsemane he experienced the emotions of rejection and pain that you have felt, and he was totally victorious. He feels for you and is with you." (Read Hebrews 5:7, which tells us what he went through to be trained as our high priest, and Hebrews 4:14-16, which tells us how much he can sympathize with all our temptations and weaknesses).

The person can now say something like this: "Thank you, God, that I went through such hard times because I was already so selfish and self-focused and spoiled. What would I have been like if I hadn't gone through this with my family? As it says in Romans 12:9, I learned to hate the evil that has happened and to cling to the good that you can bring out of the whole ordeal. Now that I have come to terms with the pain in my past, I can hold on to the good."

Ask the person, "What are some good memories you have?" Help them cling to the good as she surrenders all that was bad.

Repairing the Relationship

You may want to have the person write a letter to the one who hurt them if they are still living. If the person is not living, it may be very helpful to write the letter anyway, just to make peace with the memory of the person. Use the format of Paul when he wrote his letters to churches (except Galatians). Basically, he always started out in a very positive way. Think of this like a sandwich with the top and bottom slices of bread being the positive part: "Dear So-and-so, I really love you. I've been praying for you. I'm so thankful for you. I love the fact that we do certain things together, and I think about you a lot." And then mention all the good memories.

Say something along these lines for the middle section of the letter: "But, Dad, I also want you to know that there have been some things I have thought of lately that have really hurt me from the past. And I want you to know that I've worked through them. I don't hold them against you anymore, but this is what happened…. This is how I was feeling at the time…, but I want you to know that I forgive you and I don't hold it against you anymore. And I feel so great. I feel so free! I feel so liberated from this." (Make sure they write, "I forgive you," for this is one of the most important points you will make. If they cannot write that, they must work some more on forgiveness).

Continuing the letter, they could write something like, "Next time I come home, I'm looking forward to talking. Could we arrange to go out and have coffee together?" Or they could say, "I know you live far away, and we can't get together personally, but could I call you one Saturday so we can talk? I love you so much and want us to have a closer relationship." At the end of the letter, they should once again express love and appreciation.

Free to Grow and Help Others

End the process by praying about it, giving God the glory for the victory. God is good. They are healed and now are equipped to help others. Amen!

In closing, one additional hint is in order. If those you are trying to help have a problem getting in touch with their feelings, I recommend these books:

- *The Wounded Heart* by Dr. Dan B. Alender (workbook available also)

- *Distorted Images of God* by Dale and Juanita Ryan (helpful study to help understand where God is in all our pain)

- *Family Dysfunctions* also by the Ryans

- *Thirty Days at the Foot of the Cross* by IPI (keeps people focused on the fact that Jesus has felt every emotional abuse that you and I have ever felt)

QUESTIONS FOR THOUGHT

1. Now that you understand the whole process, has your hope for healing damaged relationships grown to offset your fears of doing it? Meditate on this.

2. Will you commit to writing out all your unresolved issues with those who have hurt you, which means bringing up some old painful feelings in order to heal?

3. Think of others whom you are pretty sure have unresolved relationship issues and tell them what you have done to resolve your hurts. Ask if you could help them do the same.

ACTION ITEMS

The action items are part and parcel of this lesson. Make a firm decision to work on yourself first and then pass it on by helping someone else deal with their issues of unforgiveness toward others.

CHAPTER THIRTY-FOUR

Where Is Your Life Headed?

—Gordon Ferguson

The way you think determines the daily course of your life. More importantly, how you think determines where you end up over the long haul. Character is built one day at a time, which means weak character can be strengthened as we make spiritual choices— and strong character can be weakened if we make unspiritual ones. "Little things mean a lot," said an old song, and certainly this is true when it comes to the effects of our thinking and actions. What seems like a small, momentary decision can lead to consequences far beyond the moment, because each decision becomes a part of shaping our characters. A rifle aimed at a target two hundred yards away may be off the mark by only a very small amount at ten feet, but when the bullet covers the distance to the target, it may miss the bull's-eye by a wide margin. The importance of making righteous decisions consistently, without becoming careless, cannot be over-stated. Your life will end up at the target toward which it is aimed now. So, when you get to where you're going, where will you be?

A Matter of Choices

How we think and how we act are tied directly to the choices we make. When speaking to young people, I never fail to address the concept of choices they have made, are presently making and will yet make. Being created in the image of God means we have the freedom of choice. It is both shameful and disheartening that we humans decide to make choices that are in stark contrast to the ones God wants us to make. But starting with Eve in the Garden, we are deceived time and time again into making selfish choices that hurt us. Think about everything God created that has life. Now consider the unfathomable truth that out of all the plants, animals, and everything else, only humans don't do what God created us to do! In all our amazing intelligence as God's crowning glory—we are the rebels. Sad, isn't it?

Beginning in childhood, many of the choices we make are consequential. We develop trends in our choice-making, and those trends develop both our character and our life's direction. Our self-ishness and unselfishness have a collective impact on our choices, which explains why Jesus said that the starting place in follow-ing him was in self-denial. Read the account in Luke 9:23: "Then he said to them all: 'Whoever wants to be my disciple must deny themselves and take up their cross daily and follow me.'" The more selfish our choices, the more damage to our character and the tra-jectory of our lives. The more unselfish our choices, the better our characters and direction will be. Simple, but not easy. The greatest of all, said Jesus, is the servant of all. It is more blessed to give than receive. Why? You are making unselfish choices, thus benefiting yourself and everyone around you. But rest assured that your life is aimed at a target, whether a good one or a bad one.

For many years, I have observed the truth of this principle in the lives of older people. Some are like the proverbial grandmother who brings cookies and milk with the sweetest of smiles. They are very warm, light-hearted, a real joy to be around. But honestly, just how many older people do you encounter who are like this? Not many, if your experience is anything like mine. The exceptions are those with Christ at the center of their lives. You see, older people have reached the target at which they have been aiming for many years, as far as character and attitudes go. The thinking which has characterized their life has now reached its full bloom, be it kind or bitter. When you get to where you're going, where will you be? Take your freedom of choice seriously.

A Matter of Thinking

Keeping our minds focused on the positive and spiritual is not easy. But with God's help, we can learn to do it. Paul provides us with an amazing example of seeing the hand of God in everything, every day. Even while chained to prison guards, he was almost beside himself with joy-filled thinking. A cursory reading of Philip-pians demonstrates this clearly. One of my favorite passages in this happy, little letter is in chapter 4:4-7: "Rejoice in the Lord always.

I will say it again: Rejoice! Let your gentleness be evident to all. The Lord is near. Do not be anxious about anything, but in every situation, by prayer and petition, with thanksgiving, present your requests to God. And the peace of God, which transcends all understanding, will guard your hearts and your minds in Christ Jesus."

Here, God tells us to rejoice, which means (1) that the choice is ours to make, and (2) we can do it. Paul is essentially saying, "Just loosen up, and trust that God is near and in control of life's circumstances." Refuse to allow the practical atheism of anxiety to control your thinking. Instead, pour out your hearts in prayer to God, bathing your heart in gratitude. Remember that the key to the future is the past; for if God has protected and provided in the past, surely he will not neglect to do so in the future. As an old man now, I appreciate more than ever the observation of David in Psalm 37:25, 28: "I was young and now I am old, yet I have never seen the righteous forsaken or their children begging bread...For the Lord loves the just and will not forsake his faithful ones."

Our Philippians passage goes on to promise us that God's peace becomes better felt than told when we have this trust in our hearts. He calls it a peace that "surpasses understanding." In other words, such a peace is better felt than described. When you have it at the deepest level, you know it, but you can't quite find the words to explain it. I don't have it nearly as often as I would like, but when I have it, I understand (and feel) exactly what Paul is describing – it transcends understanding. Just keep your mind engaged with the positives of loving and serving God and others and imitate those who have learned these lessons. Then the God of peace will be with you in life and death, for time and for eternity, during the moments of mountaintop exhilaration and during the valley-low moments of heartache and despair.

Control Your Mind

Paul goes on in the passage to point out the specific types of things on which we should keep our minds focused. "Finally, brothers and sisters, whatever is true, whatever is noble, whatever is right, whatever is pure, whatever is lovely, whatever is admirable—if anything is excellent or praiseworthy—think about such things." Okay, Paul, I hear you, but what about...? No, no, no—not those things; these things. Focus on them. We are bombarded with negativity. That is why reading the Bible is far better than reading the news. Paul finishes with the final capstone of finding godly peace in Philippians 4:9. "Whatever you have learned or received or heard from me, or seen in me—put it into practice. And the God of peace will be with you."

So, when you get to where you're going, where will you be? It all depends on the path your thinking is taking you on, day by day, month by month, year by year. Before you know it, we will all be standing before God, giving an account of how we lived our brief lives here on earth. How we feel then will be determined by how we feel now—and all feeling is a result of your thinking and doing, every day in every way. The Apostle Paul made it clear to the Christians in Rome: "Do not conform to the pattern of this world, but be transformed by the renewing of your mind. Then you will be able to test and approve what God's will is—his good, pleasing and perfect will" (Romans 12:2). The power of spiritual thinking transforms a life lived for God in this world and a soul with its Maker in eternity. Don't miss out!

QUESTIONS FOR THOUGHT

1. Do you understand how inseparably choices and character are connected? Understand and meditate on it.

2. The right kind of mind control is of God, as his principles shape your thinking. As you examine your thinking habits, how can you improve them?

3. How good do you feel about where your life is headed right now in relation to both this life and the next?

ACTION ITEMS

Write down three to five ways that you don't feel good about where your life is headed and one step to start changing each of those ways.

CHAPTER THIRTY-FIVE

You Are Not a Foster Child to God

—Gordon Ferguson

The Bible (and world history) makes it clear that we live amid a combination of good and evil. No sane person will deny that. Genesis introduces us to Satan as God's enemy who has one agenda and one alone: to fight God in every way possible. The battleground is clear. Although God created this incomprehensible universe and all its creatures, human beings are his primary focus, for they are made in his image and reflectors of his image. His focus with humans is all about relationships. As difficult as it is to believe, he wants a personal relationship with every one of us. His pursuit is so intense that he became one of us to demonstrate that focus, paying the ultimate price of dying in our place on the cross. There could be no greater sacrifice, no greater demonstration of his love.

We humans who understand the battle between good and evil, specifically between God and Satan, often contemplate and discuss how Satan works to block us from developing a personal relationship with our Creator, our Father, our Abba. The devil has many tools in his toolbox—weapons of soul destruction in his arsenal. Hebrews 4:15 informs us that Jesus was tempted in every way just as we are. First John 2:16 narrows those ways down into three broad categories: the lust of the flesh, the lust of the eyes, and the pride of life. To distill Satan's weaponry down still further, into his primary and most prized weapon, we must go back to the beginning of the battle.

Satan's Best Weapon

Satan does not mess around. Genesis 3 opens with his attack upon mankind and the introduction of his best weapon. All his supporting weapons ultimately just enhance this one: to distort our view of God through any means possible, thus destroying trust. He customizes this weapon for each of us individually so that we refuse to trust God, accept his love, or love him in return.

None of this has anything to do with God's love for us. It is unconditional and unchangeable, an ever-present reality. The problem lies on our end. From the day we are born, Satan starts his evil work against us, deceiving us about God's love for us. Satan incessantly attempts to distort our understanding of God so that we don't recognize God's immense love. As John puts it, we love because he first loved us. But until we grasp his love for us, we will not return it, and thus are blocked from the close personal relationship he so deeply longs for with each one of us.

To me, the best illustration of how deeply God longs for that relationship with us is found in the story of the Prodigal Son (Luke 15). Properly understood, this is a story about the shamed Father. Many humans have died at their own hand rather than endure a great shame that fell on them. God endured shame in the person of Jesus on the cross (Hebrews 12:2), but the entire ministry of Jesus on earth was that of bearing shame. He had no limitations on the type and amount of shame he was willing to bear to keep showing his love, for the purpose of helping us see his love and thereby be moved to return it.

A Lifelong Battle

I have been in a lifetime battle to shed my satanic distortions of God. I have figured out most of where they came from, although this took some years. Intellectually, I understand the source and the nature of those distortions, and I also understand a great deal about God's love being understood through Jesus. Jesus said that if we have seen him, we have seen the Father, for he and the Father are One (John 14:9-11). The writer of Hebrews said that "the Son is the radiance of God's glory and the exact representation of his being (Hebrews 11:1)." The Greek word *charaktēr,* suggests the idea of a minted coin, exactly like the mold in which it was formed. Hence Jesus is the exact representation of the Father. Four Gospel accounts were inspired by the Holy Spirit to make sure we "get" Jesus and therefore get God.

As I said, I think my intellectual understanding of God's nature and his purposes for my life are pretty good. Moving that understanding down into my heart and producing the emotional grasp of it has been my personal battleground. I journal my prayers each morning (at least the personal part of my prayers). Later, I pray through an extensive and ever-expanding prayer list of others in need, often dire need. Recently, I had a thought that led me to writing this piece. It was toward the end of a time journaling in the stillness of an early morning as I sat on my back patio. I had been praying for the Holy Spirit, as Jesus said we should in Luke 11:13. (This passage makes for an interesting comparison with the *almost* parallel passage in Matthew 7:7-11. You should read and compare the two.)

As I prayed for the Holy Spirit, an illustration came to me. I realized I often experience a state of mind and heart like what I imagine an emotionally abused foster child might have who has been passed from one bad parent to another. I think the analogy fits me pretty well from an emotional standpoint, in spite of obviously not having a bad heavenly Father. I also had a good earthly dad too, at least in his later years, although in my most formative early childhood years he damaged me emotionally. But the following illustration speaks to me. Perhaps it will to you also.

A New Illustration

Imagine a young boy who has been thrust into one home after another, to be cared for by parents who don't really care. He started off hoping to be accepted and loved by his foster parents, but it wasn't the case. Far from it. The next home he was assigned to found him entering the new situation with hope still, but with much less of it. A string of unmet expectations diminished his hopes, and at some point, drove it out entirely. Finally, when all hope had been destroyed, the kid enters a new home with parents who are not only determined to love him but are in fact planning on adopting him for their very own. They show him love in a myriad of ways. He can't accept it. His heart is too damaged. No trust remains. The last vestige of hope has been obliterated. He is now irreparably damaged, just waiting for the other shoe to fall and the harsh treatment to begin again. He is an utterly hopeless case. Or is he?

These parents are undeterred in their determination to show him love. His hateful responses to their loving ones don't faze them. They understand his plight. They pull out all the stops. Their patience is limitless. Day after day, week after week, month after month their demonstrations of love continue. They seem to be consumed with dreaming up new ways to show love to this hopeless child. Although it seems like everything they have done is one big failure, to them the only failure would be to give up and stop trying. That is the one thing they absolutely refuse to do.

Finally, the stack of evidence of their love is too heavy for the boy to push away. It drives him to the ground, and he feels like he is going to be crushed under its weight. Suddenly, in the twinkling of an eye, the eyes of his heart begin opening and the weight is reduced dramatically. Something is different, really different, although he doesn't understand it just yet. He soon will. When he enters the room where his parents are, they seem very different. He sees their smiles and hears their voices differently. Something stirs in his heart, something he had forgotten existed. Its name? Hope. The dawn of expectations arises once more. A big hug from his foster dad and his dammed up emotional wall collapses. Tears begin, followed by uncontrollable sobs. His sudden grasp of their love becomes a funnel through which all of their past demonstrations of love now flow into his heart like a flood. He has been born again. The impossible has become reality.

I think I have something in common with the little boy. I know the parents have something in common with God, although they only provide a dim reflection of what he is like, as amazing as they are from a human perspective. Hopefully this is another helpful illustration of the Divine love story that is too good to be true, and yet it is true. May it sink at least a little deeper into my heart, and yours. Out of his love, God sends challenges in many forms, because he knows that spiritual growth comes best through facing challenges. But as yesteryear's TV show title puts it: "Father Knows Best." Trust that and let him into your heart, again and again and again. Open the door, for he will stand at it knocking until you do.

QUESTIONS FOR THOUGHT

1. How would you describe your relationship to God on an emotional level?

2. Do you ever have trouble accepting God's love? Do you ever find yourself questioning it? Explain.

3. In what ways does the illustration of the foster child strike your heart?

ACTION ITEMS

Spend an extended period of time praying for the Holy Spirit and for Him to illuminate your heart to see from this lesson what you need to see. Write down your most profound three thoughts, then share them with someone close to you spiritually.

SECTION THREE

Additional Studies

CHAPTER THIRTY-SIX

Men Are from Mars, Women Are from Venus

—Theresa Ferguson

I heard a very wise person once say that marriages are not made in heaven; they come in kit form and must be assembled on the earth! Whatever we expected when we entered marriage, we found things different in some ways than we expected. Seeing our loved one when we were single for special, dreamy dates is quite a bit different from seeing them at 6:00 a.m. as they awaken from dreams (which might have been nightmares)! So how do we put this marriage "kit" together as God would have it?

One of the key ingredients is effective communication. This chapter's title is from a popular book demonstrating the differences in how men and women typically communicate. We will continue with the outer space analogy as we learn to better recognize our communication obstacles, figure out solutions, and take the time to make communication special.

Battle of the Planets (Communication Obstacles)

Male/Female differences are a challenge! We were with a couple who had seen a video on this topic and the husband said the title of it was "Women Are Weird!" His wife elbowed him in the ribs, saying, "Yes, and the other half of the title was, 'and Men are Strange!'" Males and females most definitely think and communicate differently. An article I read described how men tend to focus on facts and logic, whereas women tend to focus on feelings and intuition. I think that is true in our marriage and am grateful that we have both learned to appreciate our need for the other's approach.

We not only think differently; we also speak differently. Women generally give much more detail, compete with repetition and unannounced changes of channel (subjects). Women talk to figure out what is really on their minds, to work through stress and often most importantly, to develop intimacy. Until men receive a bit of training, this is rather like a foreign language to them. I love undivided attention as my main love language and having Gordon patiently and attentively listen to me talk fills my heart. Although he knows this about me, it takes a lot of effort on his part to extend both his interest and patience!

Men want to get to the bottom line quickly, for making their point is their main goal of talking in the first place. They tend to go into their "caves" to figure out that point and then emerge to announce it as quickly and succinctly as possible. Of course, if the topic is about sports or some other area of special interest, then suddenly, they delight in expounding on the details. The challenge is that such topics often are more interesting to their fellow male friends than to their wives. This means I need to strive to enter his "world" with him and show the same interest in his favorite topics as I expect him to show in mine.

The necessity of showing respect for one another in communication cannot be overstated. Do we talk to our mates in a way we would not talk to a person of the opposite sex at church? Do we talk to them in a manner differently than that used with non-Christians whom we are trying to influence? Respect is exhibited in how you listen to the other person. Are we distracted, not really listening, not focused with eye contact, just saying "uh huh" in our replies? Are we listening impatiently and simply awaiting our turn to talk?

A lack of respect in communication becomes much worse and damaging with the use of negative speech patterns. Paul's comments in Philippians 2:14-16a remind us of what such patterns really are.

"Do everything without grumbling or arguing, [15] so that you may become blameless and pure, 'children of God without fault in a warped and crooked generation.' Then you will shine among them like stars in the sky 16 as you hold firmly to the word of life."

Do you stand out like a star compared to those with whom you associate? Two bad habits seriously affect our communication: being conclusory and accusatory. The first means that we fail to seek to hear the other person's side of the story and assume way too much rather than asking to hear their side. Being accusatory means that we judge them guilty with a barb in it. "You did this, and I'll bet it was because…" It is far better to say, "It seems like this to me, but please help me understand better…" Overstatements occur when we become "historical" bringing up the past. When that happens, it is not "Always and Forever," like the romantic song, but "always" and "never!"

Our emotions so easily can get hooked. Poor communication damages the other person's feelings and may arouse anger or cause emotional retreat. Gordon tends to have "hot" wars, becoming very expressive, while I tend to have "cold" wars, stuffing my feelings and refusing to talk. Let's look in our space analogy for better answers and workable solutions.

Peaceful Planetary Alignment

Peace, harmony, and love can replace all the communication challenges we've mentioned. For starters, see the challenges (which will inevitably occur) as ways to help you grow as a person and the two of you as a couple. James 1:2-4 provides us with a valuable reminder. "[2] Consider it pure joy, my brothers and sisters, whenever you face trials of many kinds, [3] because you know that the testing of your faith produces perseverance. [4] Let perseverance finish its work so that you may be mature and complete, not lacking anything."

Mature conversation must come in the right form. It has been observed that we tend to communicate at three maturity levels: parent to child; child to parent; and adult to adult. Obviously, the latter is the goal of healthy communication in marriage. Do you ever feel like a child in your interactions with your mate? Do you ever make *them* feel like a child? The Golden Rule of Luke 6:31

should make us ask ourselves if we would appreciate receiving the same treatment we dish out?

Be humble—keep an air of fallibility; learn to say, "I'm wrong, I'm sorry, please forgive me." Honestly, practicing this one out loud together is a very worthwhile exercise. It will make it easier when the real need to apologize arises. Just keep your focus on *what* is right, not *who* is right. Learn to apologize quickly, forgive quickly, and resolve conflicts quickly.

Close Encounters of the Special Kind

First, it takes *time.* Eliminating the negatives in our communication is not the most important part; replacing it with the positives is, and it will take time. Daily emotional "touching" is a biggie. Just having a brief period of uninterrupted talking works wonders for helping our relationship stay in tune. Even better is when we end that time by praying together. Gordon and I have prayed together before bedtime for many years. They are not long prayers, but they connect us by hearing one another's hearts speaking to God.

A longer time to communicate on a weekly basis allows for longer discussions of more serious matters. Such serious discussions might not be needed in some weeks, but they might on occasion be needed even more often. I remember one evening we were getting ready to attend a Valentine's Dance and were already dressed up for it. I was troubled emotionally about something to the point that Gordon was able to sense it and ask the right questions. Thankfully, he thought spending time listening to me pour out my heart was more important than attending the dance.

Another thing we tried to do when our children were still at home is to keep the romance in our relationship by having a weekly date. Our children needed to understand that our relationship with each other as a couple took priority over our relationship with them. Without that example, how could we have expected them to get the priorities right in their eventual marriages? Expressing emotions in different ways is important—cards, flowers, texts, phone calls, etc. and the more unexpected they are, the more impact they have.

Stay young at heart and stay busy working on your relationship. Looking for new ways to celebrate your relationship is always a worthy goal. To use an analogy from a marriage program we used to teach, putting deposits in our love bank and avoiding withdrawals is an ongoing focus. No matter where you are now, just get started and take it one day at a time. Progress is the name of the game.

QUESTIONS FOR THOUGHT

1. What do you think your strengths are in communicating with your mate and what are the ones that need work?

2. What are some things you could do to make your spouse feel like they are more special to you?

3. Do you feel like your marriage, or your children are the top priority?

ACTION ITEMS

Now set up an uninterrupted discussion time with your spouse and share your answers to the three questions. Then each of you share anything else you feel compelled to talk about from the chapter.

CHAPTER THIRTY-SEVEN

Needed: Valiant Men

—Gordon Ferguson

> "Kish had a son named Saul, as handsome a young man as could be found anywhere in Israel, and he was a head taller than anyone else... Saul also went to his home in Gibeah, accompanied by valiant men whose hearts God had touched."
> (1 Samuel 9:2, 10:26)

Though he later became a great disappointment to God, in his early years Saul was truly an impressive man, a valiant warrior and king for God. He also was a man who attracted other men of valor to his leadership. We can learn important lessons from the way he lived before his heart turned in the wrong direction. Without doubt, one of the greatest needs in the kingdom of God today is for our men to be courageous and to influence other leaders in the world to join the kingdom. America has become the land of the free and the home of the wimps! It is time for every disciple to develop deep convictions and then to stand up with the power of God to live out those convictions. Strong men attract strong men, and all of us can be mighty in the power of our Almighty God.

Chosen By God

One reason behind Saul's impressive leadership was his understanding that he had been chosen by God. Because of this choosing, look what the prophet says about him: "Samuel said to all the people, 'Do you see the man the LORD has chosen? There is no one like him among all the people'" (1 Samuel 10:24). Every person in Christ's kingdom has been directly chosen by God (Ephesians 1:3-14). The fact that you are a disciple was ordained by God. He has a specific plan for your life. By his power, you can stand out in every crowd. You are unique and special, and you can be used in greater ways than you have ever dreamed if you will trust God's hand is on your life. Paul told the Ephesians: "Now to him who is able to do immeasurably more than all we ask or imagine, according to his power that is at work within us" (Ephesians 3:20). That means that within us resides resurrection power. God has provided an energy that enables us to dream big and accomplish much in advancing the kingdom of God.

Empowered by the Spirit

Another reason for Saul's success was that he was changed by the Spirit. In fact, 1 Samuel 10:6-7 alludes to this powerful encounter with the Spirit: "The Spirit of the Lord will come powerfully upon you, and you will prophesy with them; and you will be changed into a different person. Once these signs are fulfilled, do whatever your hand finds to do, for God is with you." We have the same potential for change. In Christ you change into the very image of God's Son. When you access the Spirit's power and go for the real gusto, people will take note that you are a different person! And praise God—they will be correct!

It is always helpful to compare biblical passages which appear to be parallel to one another, for occasionally you learn a striking lesson. Compare these two passages:

Matthew 7:11—"If you, then, though you are evil, know how to give good gifts to your children, how much more will your Father in heaven give good gifts to those who ask him!"

Luke 11:13—"If you then, though you are evil, know how to give good gifts to your children, how much more will your Father in heaven give the Holy Spirit to those who ask him!"

Did you notice the difference? God promises to give good gifts to those who ask, seek, and knock in this context, but he also promises to give us the Holy Spirit. I pray for the Holy Spirit daily and for gifts from him to help me live a valiant life for God.

Charge Ahead and Don't Sweat the Skeptics

Yet another factor in Saul's courage was his charitable attitude toward skeptics. When troublemakers questioned his ability to lead, he kept silent (1 Samuel 10:27). After others were ready to put the skeptics to death, Saul refused, instead calling for a focus on God (1 Samuel 11:12-13). Any man of courage in any age will be in the minority. A person in this category will not only stand out—he will be jealously attacked by others. Likewise, we must not attack our attackers. We should keep pressing the battle against the real enemy, leaving the skeptics to God. They will be discredited if we remain righteous, and they will either repent or be shamed before others. We must be willing to go against the flow of common opinion without becoming fearful or resentful.

Saul was also courageous in battle. In his first test from the enemy after he became king, he burned with anger, called his people to battle and decisively defeated the Ammonites (1 Samuel 11:1-11). He knew the Israelites could be a formidable army, and the promised land was their inheritance. The kingdom of Christ is no less powerful, although our weapons and our warfare are of a spiritual nature. We need a heightened sense of righteous indignation toward evil and a strong competitive spirit toward Satan. Men of valor love battle and hate losing! Are you such a person? Are you tired of Satan winning victories in your life and in the lives of those around you? Like Saul, we need to burn with anger and send Satan's forces into retreat (Ephesians 6:10-20).

Does this mean that we will never fear the enemy? No, for even Saul had to be coaxed out from hiding among the baggage when he was called to lead the people of God (1 Samuel 10:21-23). His famous namesake, Saul of Tarsus, sometimes preached the word in "weakness with great fear and trembling" (1 Corinthians 2:3). Despite this fear, look how God encouraged him: "One night the Lord spoke to Paul in a vision: 'Do not be afraid; keep on speaking, do not be silent. For I am with you, and no one is going to attack and harm you, because I have many people in this city.' So, Paul stayed in Corinth for a year and a half, teaching them the word of God" (Acts 18:9-11). The issue is not whether we have fear, for all people do; the issue is whether we lean on God for encouragement and keep sharing the good news, for that is something we must all do!

Enlist Other Valiant Men

Finally, Saul was a man of courage who did not hesitate to enlist others in the battle. "Whenever Saul saw a mighty or brave man, he took him into his service" (1 Samuel 14:52). Once you exert true courage, you become bold in calling others to do the same. You are able to attract bold men and help other men overcome their timidity. That is what God desires and Paul reminds his young apprentice Timothy of this: "For the Spirit God gave us does not make us timid, but gives us power, love and self-discipline" (2 Timothy 1:7). Are you attracting valiant men to the service of God? Stand up, stand out and take a stand! Be among the courageous who truly make things happen by the power of God. And unlike Saul, keep that heart all the days of your life!

QUESTIONS FOR THOUGHT

1. Do you think of yourself as having been specially chosen by God? If he chose you for salvation, do you believe he has plans beyond that for your life? What might some of them be?

2. Have you ever prayed for the Holy Spirit to be with you and in you and to do more through you than he is now doing? We are told not to quench the Spirit (1 Thessalonians 5:19, but are there ways you might be limiting the Spirit's power in your life?

3. How can you overcome fears of what others may be thinking if you begin to exert yourself toward becoming a more valiant person for God?

ACTION ITEMS

Read through the story of Saul in his younger years when he was at his best. List three to five ways that you want to imitate him and put some action steps beside them. Then get started acting upon each one.

CHAPTER THIRTY-EIGHT

Inspirational Teaching

—Theresa Ferguson

Deep in the heart of all teachers should be the compelling desire to make a real difference in the lives of our students, which include our own children and grandchildren. Thinking back through my life, as I was taught about God, Jesus and the Bible as a child, I recall with great appreciation certain teachers who made an eternal impact on my heart. They did not view teaching children as a menial task that someone had to do; they saw it as an opportunity to plant spiritual seeds that would produce fruit for a lifetime and change the destiny of souls. The end result in my life was far-reaching indeed. I majored in Elementary Education in college and taught in the public school system. I taught Bible classes in a traditional church for many years and taught my own children daily when they lived with me. (Now I am teaching my grandchildren!) My teachers inspired me to teach.

Can you think of teachers who had a similar impact on your heart and life? Take some time to think about it as you read this chapter. If you can still remember certain teachers, they were truly inspirational, as were the lessons they taught you. Being *effective* teachers demands that we are *inspirational teachers*. This is not an option.

Imitating the Master

Inspirational teaching—what is it? According to the dictionary, to inspire others means "to fill with an animating, quickening, or exalting influence; to influence or impel; to animate, as an influence, feeling, thought, or the like, to prompt or instigate by influence." For us, it means we have imitated Jesus enough to teach like he taught. It also means we have imitated the effective teachers he has put in our lives.

What can we learn from Jesus, the Master Teacher? He was inspired by God to the point that he totally loved the word of God and the people for whom it was written. He so loved the God's message that he made it come alive to all who heard his teaching. All inspirational teaching begins with a teacher who loves God, God's word and the ones whom he or she is laboring to teach. In the practical aspects of teaching, Jesus was unexcelled. The task of the teacher is to know the subject well enough to break it down into easily understood parts and to make the presentation captivating. Look how Jesus did this:

1. He used simple illustrations from everyday life.

2. He asked many questions, both to prompt thinking and to see if he was being understood.

3. He made applications and called for responses.

4. He demonstrated his teaching, as in the case when he washed the disciples' feet (John 13).

Without doubt, Jesus labored to make God's message clearly understood. How much effort do you make in planning your lessons to ensure that you are both practical and inspirational? Such teaching does not "just happen." It comes at a price, and we must be willing to pay the price.

Lasting Impact

Don't ever doubt the difference you can make. The most exciting and inspiring teacher I can remember from my childhood had an amazing impact on me when I was 8 years old. In fact, my desire to help others to know God traces back to what she said in one particular presentation to my class. She made me believe that sharing God's word was the most important thing anyone could possibly do with their lives. I can still remember much of what inspired me from that one class. She captured the attention of the class by turning out the lights in the room and held a candle to provide light. She entered the room dressed like a woman from the country about which she was sharing. She acted out what she would do in that country to share Jesus with the children there, and then urged us to share with our friends, making the point that unless we shared, they would never know about Jesus. I made a decision that day in response to her inspiring presentation and God has helped me carry out that dream, even to the point of teaching people in other countries about him!

Note the inspirational principles that this teacher used so effectively:

1. She made sure that our eyes, hearts and minds were drawn into her presentation.

2. Her dress provided a very effective visual aid to help us connect with the situation she described.

3. Her words were brief but appropriate for the age level and were delivered with dramatic intensity and conviction.

4. She made her message applicable to us in a way that left us knowing exactly how to put it into practice in our lives.

5. She held the Bible so that we all could see it, and the way she handled it made us realize its exalted importance.

6. She instilled confidence in us that God had a plan for our lives and would use us to change the world.

7. Finally, she called for a decision and response to her lesson. That I remember so much detail about her convictions, her life and her presentation for almost half a century shows the power of a teacher to inspire and change the lives of impressionable children.

Practical Applications

Let me close by giving you some practical tools and tips for teaching children today:

1. Remember that 70% of your influence as a teacher will be the manner of your interaction with the children. Do you love them? Are you making it real and fun?

2. Prepare your mind and heart by letting the Bible inspire

you. Read the story you are going to present many times, visualizing it in your mind to make it come alive to you, and then thinking of ways to make it come alive to your students.

3. Pray for each child every day by name. Keep a list of their names handy in your Bible.

4. Realize that spirits communicate with spirits, which means that the children (even the very young) will definitely sense how important they are to you and how important effective communication with them actually is. Your excitement and personal involvement will make or break the effectiveness of the class.

5. Think about the kind of preaching and teaching that inspires and motivates you most and pattern your own teaching after these same principles that others use effectively.

6. Understand that inspiring the children begins with your initial greeting of the children as they enter the class. Eye contact and the use of exciting, encouraging words set the stage for the rest of the class. In the pre-class portion, asking the children about their day and making personalized comments about their feelings or appearance helps to pull them in emotionally. ("Johnny, I am so happy to see you today. We are going to have such an exciting Bible story about Jonah!")

7. In presenting the Bible Story section, the use of animation with exaggerated movement of the arms, hands and eyes is absolutely essential for gaining and keeping attention. Self-denial and focusing on the children will help you to lose your own inhibitions and self-consciousness.

8. Appeal to their five senses (sight, touch, smell, taste, hearing) to keep them involved in what you are communicating. Food to smell and taste, bright colored pictures to see, action songs to sing and hear, and toys and visuals to touch are all effective ways to keep yourself and the children animated and connected emotionally.

9. Make the most of every opportunity, realizing that every minute can be used to influence the children toward spiritual values that will change their lives.

10. Use the Scriptures. Keep the Bible open and let the children interact with the Bible.

11. Use personal examples, stating your love for God and the Bible and calling on the other teachers to do the same. Asking fellow teachers, "Do you love the Bible?" will provide a model for the students to imitate.

12. Call the children to a decision by asking them for a reply—"Will you love Jesus and tell others about him?"

What an opportunity we all have! In any given class we can do and say things that children will remember for a lifetime. Let us pray that we will not waste these precious opportunities but will make an inspiring imprint on the young hearts and minds that are entrusted to us.

QUESTIONS FOR THOUGHT

1. Can you think of teachers in a school or church setting who impacted you greatly?

2. Although this lesson is aimed at teaching in the classroom, what can you apply to teaching your family at home (children, grandchildren and other relatives)?

3. Which points in the lesson stand out most to you? Will you begin applying them?

ACTION ITEMS

Share this lesson with others who have young children at home and/or teach classes in a church setting. Discuss specific ways to put the lessons into practice.

CHAPTER THIRTY-NINE

As Your Parents Age...

—Theresa Ferguson

I recently reflected on when Gordon and I were dealing with the aging and deaths of our parents, and a myriad of thoughts and feelings came to the surface. I've laughed and cried as I've written this, but it has been good for me to think through it all again. Expressing feelings with pen and paper (or on electronics) is therapeutic and good for the soul. As your parents age, going through various stages and then passing into eternity, you will be left with many feelings. The better you express them, the better you will be able to process your experiences and come to peace with whatever you are facing at any stage of the journey.

There have been many occasions when I have sat across from people who were dealing with their aging and dying parents. The flow of this chapter is what I follow when talking through this subject with others. There's no cookie-cutter method to having sensitive talks like these, so I vary the order based on what the person I am sharing with feels the need to discuss most. Then I make sure that I cover the other aspects of the subject as well, for I am convinced that all are important.

The Reality of the Aging Process

First, let's discuss the reality of the aging process. When I share with someone about the aging process, I always share 2 Corinthians 4:16, which reads: "Therefore we do not lose heart. Though outwardly we are wasting away, yet inwardly we are being renewed day by day." Our bodies are aging with wrinkles, weakening muscles, less energy, deterioration of the inner organs during illnesses, and ongoing health challenges. Facing the truth about this description from God's word is so hard when we experience it firsthand with our aging parents. My father died suddenly, and we were not around Gordon's father often during his final decline. Both our mothers aged and died in very different ways, and some of the material I will now share with you comes from what I experienced with those wonderful women whom I miss dearly.

My mother died with congestive heart failure after having undergone two open heart surgeries. She could not survive a third. She was determined to remain as active as possible and did. She was outwardly focused on the needs of others, which was most gratifying for me and my family. My mother and I enjoyed a deep relationship all my life, and in some ways, she was more like a sister and friend than simply a mother. To the very end, she remained who she always was, refusing to retreat into a shell.

My mother-in-law was also like a true mother to me. I met her when I was a young teenager, and she was a special friend to me from the very beginning of my relationship with Gordon. (I like to say that we "chose each other" when Gordon and I first started dating.) During the last part of her life, she developed a rare form of palsy that robbed her (and us) of who she had always been. The deterioration of her body brought many of her weaknesses to the surface, and these hurt most of us in the family. It was almost like she was already gone, so our grieving process started long before she died. It was both a confusing and hurtful thing to experience. Her condition wasn't dementia but affected her and us much the same. The mother we knew was gone.

During her last few years, she lived near Gordon's sister, Pam, but was occasionally able to visit us before the disease fully took her over. When she was with us, I made the sacrifices that were needed, including changing her diapers, bathing her, and caring for her every need. I rubbed her head, which once was filled with beautiful blonde hair, but was then covered with thin white hair and large knots under the scalp. I also massaged her deformed feet that once were busy serving me and our family. We reminisced about all the fun times and about the countless ways she served all of us in the family. When she felt awkward about me changing her diapers, I reminded her of the ways she took care of me after my two miscarriages and other surgeries. I kept reminding her how I cherished every minute that I had with her.

I had to learn when she treated me in a hurtful way not to take it personally. I apologized when I didn't respond well, but on the other hand, I refused to be manipulated by her hurtful words and actions. When we were together, I really listened to her and empathized with her aches, pains and unhappiness. I prayed to treat her as if she were Jesus, regardless of her actions and words. I continued to remind her of the good things that she had done for us in the past, often through cards mentioning specific instances of her loving kindness.

The Reality of Death and Judgment

Facing the reality of a parent's aging is much the same emotionally as facing their death, and we go through the same stages of grief. First comes shock and denial, as we realize that the old days are gone and there is no going back. Second, the stage of anger may come in as we grow to resent the changes. We are tempted to be angry at the person, at the aging process, and maybe at God himself. Third, the feelings of guilt and depression come as we think back to what we should or could have done, and to what we are doing or failing to do now. Fourth, the stage of acceptance must finally be reached as we work through those earlier stages. Wherever our parents may be in the aging process, we know that death is destined to be the ultimate outcome of it.

I experienced all those stages personally in a deep way through facing the aging and death of so many of my closest relatives. Reaching closure has not always been easy nor quick, but one thing that really helped was to write each of them a long letter after their death, in which I evaluated our relationship and worked through my feelings about them. I had to also face the truth about the uncertainties in several cases regarding their spiritual destinies and my own regrets about what I wish I had done to help them more. Those painful considerations helped me to plan and carry out my good intentions with those who were still alive.

One of my best victories was in helping my mother face her own death and judgment before God. It began as one of my greatest challenges but ended as one of my greatest joys. The memories of that experience will be cherished forever. I expressed to her that one of my deepest regrets was that she wasn't going to be with me in heaven. This led to our studying the Bible again, and one of my greatest joys is that she is going to be with me in heaven! As a child, she was the one who first taught me to love God, and as an adult, I was blessed to be able to teach her what really loving God biblically was all about. My brother, Curt, his wife, Janet, their son, Ian and I were able to baptize her into Christ in February of 2001, before she passed in November of 2002. I want to encourage you that even if your parents or close relatives do not initially respond to your outreach positively, don't give up trying to reach them until they take their last breath.

The Reality of the Blessings Left Behind

Don't let the blessings of the past be diminished by the challenges of the present. I have purposed to hold on to the good qualities, skills and experiences from all four of our parents with which I have been blessed. I want the blessings from those special relationships to continue in and through my life when the people are no longer with me. I assured them while they were alive how much those things meant to me and how I would never let those things die. I mentioned many specifics of what they had taught me in as much detail as I could remember.

No matter how useless our parents felt in their weakened conditions, I wanted to make sure that they knew that their impact would be passed on through my children and grandchildren even after I'm gone. I tell my children and grandchildren where I learned to do the things for them that I am doing, and I ask them to pass it on to their children after them. I can do nothing to stop the natural process of aging and dying, but through God's power, I can make the process a positive one. Praise God that we don't "grieve like the rest of mankind, who have no hope" (1 Thessalonians 4:13), whether it is the grief that comes through the aging process or through death itself!

It is comforting to know that God is feeling with us in these ultimate realities and has promised to reward our faith as we cling to him in trying times. As I close out, I urge you to meditate on two passages that have helped me most through those trying times – Hebrews 4:14-16 and 2 Corinthians 1:3-5.

QUESTIONS FOR THOUGHT

1. Parents usually hit stages where the aging process really kicks in. Have either of your parents or any of your in-laws hit this stage, and if yes, how are you handling it?

2. If you have already lost a parent or an in-law, are you processing it well? What from this chapter helps you to process your feelings even more effectively?

3. The pain of grief must give way to the blessings of memories. The temptation is to skip grieving and experience the blessing, though. Grief must be dealt with thoroughly. How are you doing with this balance and what do you need to change?

ACTION ITEMS

Spend some time journaling about your feelings dealing with the inevitabilities of your parents aging and dying. Share this with a close friend who has faced these things before you and get help in handling your own process the best way.

CHAPTER FORTY

Righteous Leadership

—Gordon Ferguson

"Flee the evil desires of youth and pursue righteousness, faith, love and peace, along with those who call on the Lord out of a pure heart. Don't have anything to do with foolish and stupid arguments, because you know they produce quarrels. And the Lord's servant must not be quarrelsome but must be kind to everyone, able to teach, not resentful. Opponents must be gently instructed, in the hope that God will grant them repentance leading them to a knowledge of the truth, and that they will come to their senses and escape from the trap of the devil, who has taken them captive to do his will." (2 Timothy 2:22-26)

As a leader, nothing is more important than possessing and demonstrating personal righteousness. It is what opens others up to receiving our message of Jesus. It is what gives us the confidence to call others to follow our leadership. It is the example that draws them to want to imitate our faith, as Hebrews 13:7 says: "Remember your leaders, who spoke the word of God to you. Consider the outcome of their way of life and imitate their faith." It is what sustains us when no one else is around to monitor us except God alone. Truly, righteousness is important enough to *pursue* every day in every way. All the charisma, talent, and ministry skills in the world will end up as rubbish without personal righteousness. While we may cover up unrighteousness in the short run and appear successful, God will ultimately expose our sins and humble us before others.

Our level of righteousness is constantly being tested by Satan. Although the tests come in many forms, how we deal with opposition is an especially important one. The above quotation from 2

Timothy is immediately followed by this very subject. Verses 23-26 are among the most significant in the New Testament regarding how to maintain righteous leadership in the face of resistance and rejection. If I had to pick out one passage about righteous communication in the entire Bible, this would be it. The principles found in it are simple (not easy) but profound.

Avoid Foolish and Stupid Arguments

First, Paul warns us not to have anything to do with arguments and quarrels. He calls such practices "foolish" and "stupid." You may win a debate and lose a disciple in the process. Arguments are produced by the pride of wanting to be *right* rather than *righteous*. We get caught up in *who* is correct rather than *what* is correct. Jesus spoke truth in love quite forcefully without getting hooked into ungodly emotional reactions. Aroused tempers are an indication of self-concern instead of a genuine concern for others.

Jim McCartney, one of my most treasured friends, has given me so many good insights of wisdom from his own walk with God. Jim told me: "The older I get, beyond a set of core convictions I have about God and life, I often don't have an absolute answer and am open to learning and developing how I think about different topics. I have grown to appreciate qualities like humility, effort, kindness, grace, respect, desire, and love more than the ability to be persuasive or to win." (Jim McCartney in his article, "What is Truth?" See on mccartneyjim.blogspot.com)

Paul's remedy for avoiding quarrels is three-fold. First, be kind to everyone. Be kind to your enemies (love them, in fact —Matthew 5:44). Be kind to other disciples. Be kind to your children and to your spouse. Read 1 Corinthians 13:4-8 and ask yourself how consistently you are loving the people God has put in your life. Also, ask how well you demonstrate these qualities when you are being opposed. That is the most accurate gauge of who you really are.

1 Corinthians 13:4-8

Love is patient, love is kind. It does not envy, it does not boast, it is not proud. ⁵ It does not dishonor others, it is not self-seeking, it is not easily angered, it keeps no record of wrongs. [6] Love does not delight in evil but rejoices with the truth. [7] It always protects, always trusts, always hopes, always perseveres. [8] Love never fails...

Second, Paul commands us to gently instruct those who oppose us. That is a far cry from the approach followed by unrighteous leaders. They are fond of hammering people to force them to repent. Even though Jesus never forced anyone to do the right thing, some apparently believe they can do better than he did. Our job is to present truth in the correct way—the other person's responsibility is to accept or reject it and experience the consequences either way. Righteous leaders respect people's freedom to choose for themselves.

I had some pictures on top of my chest of drawers leaning against the wall, which left marks on the wall. Fortunately, I had some of the original paint stored in a bathroom cabinet and knew it would blend into the existing paint when covering the marks. There were many blemishes to paint over, and I looked for them carefully, even using a flashlight to make sure I didn't miss any. I didn't. My purpose involved a process of only looking for flaws and correcting them. Similarly, some leaders believe that looking only for flaws is their job. That approach to leading people is horrific and does damage beyond imagination. Trying to force righteous behavior in others only proves your own unrighteousness as a leader.

Third, focus on your own demeanor and not that of the one opposing you. They are, according to this passage, out of their senses. Of course their manner is going to be unrighteous! Don't you dare just turn it back on them, accusing them of pride and defensiveness! Your job is to help them, not hurt them. Treating someone who is out of their senses as if they are not is a guaranteed path to failure. Just remember that this is a battle between them and Satan, not between you and them, with God trying to use you as his vessel to stop the damage.

Fourth, we do our teaching in kindness with the hope that God will grant the opposition repentance. Only he can bring about repentance. Immature leaders force issues because they think it is all up to them. Righteous leaders maintain a calm demeanor because they know that it is ultimately up to God. They do their part and leave the results in God's more than capable hands. This frees the one we are correcting to respond to God instead of responding to our temper or unkind approach.

Are you a righteous leader? Your treatment of those who oppose you helps determine the answer to that question. In view of 2 Timothy 2:23-26, how well are you doing as a leader? It is time to pursue God's brand of righteous leadership!

QUESTIONS FOR THOUGHT

1. Prior to reading this piece, how might you have defined a righteous leader? How might you define it differently now?

2. What can you think about in the midst of someone opposing you, perhaps quite strongly, to stay calm and let the Holy Spirit do his work on them? It is wise to have a plan prior to such situations.

3. Think of times when leaders did not follow Paul's admonition here to Timothy and how it made you feel. Now think of times when leaders did follow his admonition and how it made you feel.

ACTION ITEMS

Try to recall the people with whom you may have had the most serious conflicts over the past decade and examine how closely you followed God's teaching in 2 Timothy 2. When you think of times you didn't handle opposition righteously, get back to them (in person when possible) and read this passage and apologize for the ways you didn't follow its principles.

Books by Gordon Ferguson
available at
www.ipibooks.com

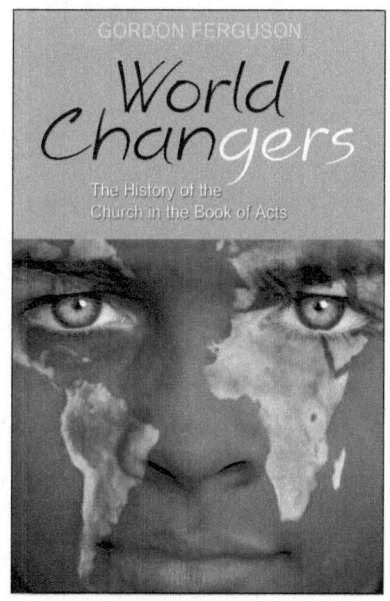

Welcome to the New

ILLUMINATION
PUBLISHERS
www.ipibooks.com

Illumination Publishers International
www.ipibooks.com